10/02

PRESENTING

Mildred D. Taylor

Twayne's United States Authors Series
Young Adult Authors

Patricia J. Campbell, General Editor

TUSAS 714

MILDRED TAYLOR'S FAMILY IN FRONT OF
THEIR FAMILY HOME IN 1901.

Courtesy Mildred D. Taylor.

PRESENTING

Mildred D. Taylor

Chris Crowe

Twayne Publishers
New York

Twayne's United States Authors Series No. 714

Presenting Mildred D. Taylor
Chris Crowe

Twayne Publishers
1633 Broadway
New York, NY 10019

Library of Congress Cataloging-in-Publication Data
Crowe, Chris.
    Presenting Mildred D. Taylor / Chris Crowe
        p. cm. — (Twayne's United States authors series; TUSAS
    714. Young adult authors)
    Includes bibliographical references and index.
    ISBN 0–8057–1687–4 (alk. paper)
    1. Taylor, Mildred D. — Criticism and interpretation. 2. Young
adult fiction, American—History and criticism. 3. Historical
fiction, American—History and criticism. 4. Domestic fiction,
American—History and criticism. 5. Afro-American families in
literature. 6. Afro-Americans in literature. 7. Race relations in
literature. 8. Mississippi—In literature. 9. Racism in
literature. I. Title. II. Series: Twayne's United States authors
series; TUSAS 714. III. Series: Twayne's United States authors
series. Young adult authors.
PS3570.A9463Z64 1999
813'.54—dc21   99-25527
                                                              CIP

This paper meets the requirements of ANSI/NISO Z3948-1992
(Permanence of Paper).
10 9 8 7 6 5 4 3 2

Printed in the United States of America

For Carrie and Joanne:

I hope the Taylors and the Logans will inspire you
as they have me.

Contents

Preface

Mildred D. Taylor hasn't always been one of my favorite authors. I had studied young adult literature for a long time and had heard plenty about her work, especially the 1977 Newbery Award winning *Roll of Thunder, Hear My Cry* (1976), but somehow I managed to ignore or avoid reading it. Friends and colleagues regularly recommended her book; it was often cited in critical articles and sources, and those citations were always positive.

Still, it took me a long time to finally open the pages of *Roll of Thunder, Hear My Cry*. One of my excuses, perhaps the most flimsy of them, was that I was very busy reading other books, books that had come out in the late 1980s and 1990s. And knowing, as I did, that Taylor's more recent books were sequels to *Roll of Thunder,* I figured I couldn't/shouldn't read those until I read *Roll of Thunder.* Looking back now on my avoidance of *Roll of Thunder,* I think part of my reluctance had to do with some biases I had as a reader and a person. As a reader, I was initially put off by the paperback cover of the novel. Yes, I know—and have frequently preached—that we shouldn't judge books by their covers, but as a middle-aged man, I wasn't too interested in reading a book that featured a nine-year-old girl on the cover. The Newbery Award worked against the book as well. As a specialist in literature for young adults, I had noticed that many of the Newbery Award books seemed targeted for a juvenile, preteen audience. Knowing so little about *Roll of Thunder,* I assumed that, good as the book might be, it really wasn't in the age range that I'm most interested in. And, finally, I had read a handful of historical novels about African Americans, and the few that I had sampled weren't all that satisfying.

So I remained blind to Taylor and her work for too many years.

My eyes were finally opened when, at the insistence of a trusted colleague, I included *Roll of Thunder, Hear My Cry* in my required reading for a young adult literature course I was teaching. That meant I would have to read it too.

And I did, caught up by Cassie Logan's narrative, from "Little Man, would you come on? You keep it up and you're going to make us late" to "I cried for T.J. For T.J. and the land." Taylor's book, Cassie's story, gripped me as few other novels had. Initially, Taylor's strong, admirable characters and the story of the Logan's struggles against oppression appealed to me simply as a reader. What reader would not be captured by the suspense and tension that grew out of every chapter? Who would not feel horror, shame, and regret while reading of the terrible injustices that existed in Mississippi in the 1930s? Who would not be interested in Cassie and T.J., or in the mysterious Mr. Morrison and Jeremy? Who could help admiring Mr. Jamison and loathing the Simms?

As I prepared to teach *Roll of Thunder, Hear My Cry,* I began to look beyond the novel's most basic appeal, but I found that as I examined the novel more closely, it was impossible for me to separate my personal response from my critical response. The two aspects of the book that I found most appealing were the portrayal of family and the historical detail of the racism African Americans in the South had to endure. I supposed that some of my students would say these are at opposing ends of an aesthetic spectrum, but I didn't care. I envied and admired the Logans' loving, unified family and was horrified by the brutal treatment they and their neighbors endured. Those would be the two strands from which we would study the novel, and if my students didn't like it, tough. Fortunately—for me and for them—they loved the novel, and they also chose, without any prodding from me, to study its family and historical perspectives.

While doing some background reading for teaching, I discovered that although *Roll of Thunder, Hear My Cry* was Taylor's best-known work, it wasn't her first. Her first book, *Song of the Trees* (1975), was itself an award-winning book and the beginning of the Logan family cycle. After a little searching, I tracked down

Song of the Trees, a surprisingly thin little book and zipped through it. In it, I saw the same themes and values I appreciated in *Roll of Thunder,* recognized the same narrative voice and the same characters, but missed the depth of plot that Taylor developed in *Roll of Thunder.* Still, I liked the book and was happy to have discovered it.

In the years that followed, I continued to teach *Roll of Thunder, Hear My Cry* and noted, from time to time, that Taylor had come out with yet another book. I didn't pay much attention to these, other than to add them and the awards they won to my lecture notes. Despite the positive reviews her subsequent books received, I was sure that I'd be disappointed. What could possibly compare to *Roll of Thunder?* And knowing that the "sophomore jinx" applies equally in writing as it does in sports, I was sure that after her Newbery effort, even Taylor wouldn't be able to maintain her quality.

A few years later, I discovered I was wrong. Her sequels to *Roll of Thunder, Let the Circle Be Unbroken* (1981) and *The Road to Memphis* (1990) and the two spin-offs from the Logan family series, *The Friendship* (1987) and *Mississippi Bridge* (1990), were every bit as engaging and interesting as *Roll of Thunder* had been. Her autobiographical children's book, *The Gold Cadillac* (1987) captured, in a short text, the same family values and historical tensions that are woven throughout the Logan books. My most recent find was *The Well: David's Story* (1995), a prequel to the Logan family books, with Cassie's father as the young protagonist. Every one of her books has interested and moved me, and with each one I became a more and more ardent fan of Mildred D. Taylor.

Not long ago, Patricia Campbell, general editor of this Twayne Young Adult Author series, asked me if I would be interested in writing a book for it. She named a handful of authors, including Mildred D. Taylor, whom she felt were appropriate for a study combining biography and literary criticism and asked which author I'd be most interested in working on. After I overcame the euphoria I felt at being invited to write a book for this prestigious series, I carefully considered the various authors Patty had suggested. All of them were familiar to me, and several were favorites of mine, but as I considered the time and work involved in writing a book and my own interests and values, I realized that I really had no choice at all. In my estimation, the quality of Taylor's work far exceeded that of the other authors on the list, but more significant, I felt that Taylor and I shared the same values: family is important, racism is evil and corruptive, and writers for young people have an obligation to tell the truth and to present important values to their readers. The decision made, I called Patty and told her I wanted to do the book on Taylor. After reviewing my formal proposal for this book, she and the Twayne editors agreed, and the work was set in motion.

The English department at my university assigned a graduate student, Shauna Barnes, to me as a research assistant, and I immediately sent her to the library with instructions to "find everything ever written by or about Mildred D. Taylor." She also searched for background materials on the civil rights movement, Emmett Till, and other tangential historical materials. I also asked Shauna to read all of Taylor's books so we could discuss them together.

About this same time, I began informal research on Taylor. I let people know I was working on a book about the famous Newbery author and at conferences asked colleagues what they knew about her and if they had ever met her or heard her speak. Everyone, of course, knew Taylor's work, especially *Roll of Thunder, Hear My Cry,* but I met only two people who had ever seen her in person. Initially, I was surprised. Most successful young adult authors spend at least a little time on the lecture circuit, but the more I talked to people in the young adult literature business, the more it began to seem that Taylor was an exception to that rule.

No problem, I thought. I'll build a solid research base from printed materials. Surely there would be plenty of material about Mildred D. Taylor and her books. Unfortunately, the background biographical research that Shauna and I were compiling soon revealed a pattern: nearly all the works that dealt with biographical information on Mildred D. Taylor cited the same handful of sources. In addition, Taylor had made few speeches, and only a few of those were available in print. It was becoming obvious, painfully obvious, that although a solid body of critical sources on Taylor's writing were available, most of my work on her biography would have to come from interviews. The dearth of biographical information also made it clear that, most likely, Taylor enjoyed her privacy. Fine, I thought, she's a private person. I'm a private person. We'll get along quite well.

It was time to go to the source herself to continue my research, so I called Taylor's longtime editor and friend, Phyllis Fogelman at Dial Books, to explain my project, to find out where Mildred D. Taylor lived and how I could contact her, and to gather whatever information she might be able to give me. After I introduced myself and explained a little about the Twayne Young Adult Author Series and my own project on Mildred D. Taylor, Fogelman and I chatted for a while about Taylor's writing, what she was currently working on, and about how much we both admired the author and her books. Fogelman has worked with Taylor since 1973 and knows her well. She told me that Taylor loves her family and loves her work, but that in recent years she has shunned the spotlight. How was I planning to write this book? she asked.

"Well," I said, "when Patty Campbell wrote her book on Robert Cormier, he and his wife invited her to visit their home for a few days to conduct interviews and to get to know him better."

"Don't expect to do that."

"Oh, no," I said, "I'm not planning on living in her home or anything like that. I would like to meet her in person some time, but I think I could conduct most of the research I need in a few telephone interviews."

Fogelman told me she would contact Taylor about my project to see if she would be willing to participate. I then told Fogelman I'd send her a copy of the most recent Twayne book, *Presenting Gary Paulsen,* along with my proposal and a letter introducing myself and describing how I hoped this book would turn out. I asked her to review these materials and then to forward them to Taylor to help her understand me and my project. Fogelman was enthusiastic about the book and the positive attention it would bring to her most notable author and promised to send my materials to Taylor as soon as she received them.

A few days later, I mailed the materials to Fogelman at Dial Books, looking forward to hearing back from her, or even better, from Mildred D. Taylor herself.

Days, weeks, even a couple of months passed: No word from Taylor. No word from Fogelman. I didn't want to contact Taylor directly, especially now that I knew how much she valued her privacy; I wanted to respect her wishes, and besides, intrusive or premature contact might alienate or annoy her and eliminate any chance I might have of talking with her. Besides that, I didn't have a phone number or address for her. I didn't want to badger the famous editor and risk alienating my only potential ally in making contact with Mildred D. Taylor, but at the same time, I wanted to get to work on this project. I was stuck in a situation where I really could do nothing.

In the months that followed, I continued my research on Taylor, directing my attention to her books, reading each one several times, making notes in the margins, underlining passages, writing down cross-references among the books. Occasionally, I'd find a new source on her to add to my file, but the work went slowly because I believed that I should put off starting until I heard from Taylor. Every few months, I'd follow up on my work by calling Fogelman or a publicist at Dial Books to see if Taylor had yet decided to talk to me. No, not yet. Fine. I went back to work, work that I was enjoying more each day.

More time passed without word from Taylor. Some people might have become frustrated, but as I learned more and more about her, the fact that I couldn't contact her didn't bother me; I wasn't at all surprised that she hadn't called yet. Why? Well for starters, this book certainly wasn't Taylor's idea, it was mine. And as a successful, established author, Taylor doesn't really want or need the publicity a book like this brings. As I continued working, I assumed that her priorities lay elsewhere—in her writing, her family, and her personal life—not in promoting herself or her work, and I admired that about her. Her work says what it says, means what it means. She had already done the hard work of producing her books and probably wanted to let her books speak for themselves. The fact that I had no contact with Taylor during my early work on this book turned out to be beneficial because it forced me to concentrate on her books, not on her life.

With my deadline looming I made up my mind to start writing without any interviews. By then, I knew enough about Taylor and more than enough about her books to get to work. So I did. And not long after I had started writing, I made up my mind that this would be a fine book even without any interviews with Taylor. Knowing her as I felt I did, I also decided that I really didn't want to intrude on her privacy to finish my work. She deserved to be left alone if that's what she wanted.

The more time I spent studying her books, reading about the Taylor family, and writing about Taylor and her books, the more I admired her stories and her family. As a writer, I wished I could write as beautifully as she does. As a human being, I found myself wishing many times that my own family could be as unified and close as hers. As a father, I wished I could be as wise, noble, and courageous as her own father and as the character based on her father, David Logan. As my admiration grew, I had a stronger desire than ever to meet Taylor, but not to interview her or to solicit her help with this book; I wanted to meet her simply because of what she and her stories had come to mean to me.

Ever the optimist, I felt confident that one day I'd find a letter from her in my mailbox or answer the phone one day and hear, "Hello, Chris? This is Mildred Taylor." That would be the beginning of some delightful conversations with a delightful woman about her life and her books. Those conversations would help me appreciate her novels more than ever before, an appreciation I might share with many readers through this Twayne book.

Or maybe I'd keep them to myself.

Anyway, I knew it was very likely that I would never have the good fortune to meet Mildred D. Taylor in person, and it was also possible that not only would I not meet her, but I might never even hear from her. In that case, this book would be my earnest effort to construct for readers the Mildred D. Taylor I have come to know and admire through study, research, and reading.

On a sunny morning in February, one day after I had finished my first complete draft of this book, the phone rang.

"Hello, Chris? This is Mildred Taylor."

Ah, dreams do come true.

She very graciously apologized for not getting in touch with me sooner, explaining what I already knew, that she is a very private person. She then thanked me for my letters and my patience and asked what she could do to help. I asked her a few questions and gave her a brief overview of this project, promising to send a copy of the manuscript as soon as it was presentable. But then we talked for nearly an hour about my book, her books, my family, her family. It was a wonderful conversation, and I couldn't have asked for a more fitting reward for my months of hard work on this project.

And the best part? We would talk again.

But even if Mildred D. Taylor had never called, this book would have been a labor of love. Who could ask for better work than to spend many months wallowing in fine books and studying the life of a talented author and wonderful person?

Acknowledgments

This book could not have been written without the skillful and thorough library research done by graduate research assistant, Shauna Barnes; the support of the English Department and College of Humanities at Brigham Young University; the assistance of Phyllis Fogelman of Dial Books; the direction and thorough feedback of my editor Patty Campbell; and the kind and generous cooperation of Mildred D. Taylor. I am also indebted to the many others who have helped in various ways on this project.

My heartfelt love and thanks go to my wife, Elizabeth, for her patience, encouragement, and suggestions as I studied and wrote about Mildred D. Taylor. To Christy, Jonathan, Carrie, and Joanne, thank you for letting me take some time away from you to spend on this book. You mean more to me than any book ever could.

All photographs are used courtesy of Mildred D. Taylor.

Permission to quote excerpts from the following material has been granted courtesy Mildred D. Taylor: ALAN Award Acceptance speech; *Boston Globe/Horn Book* Award speech; "Growing Up with Stories"; Newbery Medal Acceptance speech; and *Roll of Thunder, Hear My Cry*.

The author also gratefully acknowledges permission to quote an excerpt from: "Mildred D. Taylor," by Fogelman, Phyllis J., *The Horn Book Magazine*, August 1977, reprinted by permission of The Horn Book, Inc., 11 Beacon St., Suite 1000, Boston, MA 02108.

Chronology

1943 Mildred Delois Taylor born 13 September in Jackson, Mississippi. Family moves to Toledo, Ohio, when she is four months old.

1953 Family moves to a newly integrated neighborhood in Toledo. Taylor enrolls in an integrated school for the first time.

1954 31 May, Supreme Court ruling, *Brown* v. *Board of Education* of Topeka, mandates school integration.

1955 28 August, Emmett Till murdered in Mississippi. 1 December, Rosa Parks refuses to give up her seat on a bus in Montgomery, Alabama.

1957 Enters Scott High School, Toledo, Ohio. 23 September, nine black students integrate Central High School in Little Rock, Arkansas.

1961 Enrolls in the University of Toledo.

1962 Writes *Dark People, Dark World* under pen name "M. D. Taylor."

1965 Earns bachelor's degree in education from the University of Toledo. Works as English and history teacher in Tuba City, Arizona.

1965–1967 Goes to Ethiopia as a Peace Corps worker.

1967–1968 Works as Peace Corps recruiter in Chicago; instructor in Peace Corp training camp in Maine.

1968 Enrolls in the University of Colorado in September.

1969	Earns master of arts degree in journalism from University of Colorado. Helps establish the Black Studies Program at the University of Colorado.
1970–1971	Works as study skills coordinator, University of Colorado. Spends the summer of 1970 in Ethiopia.
1971	Moves to Los Angeles, California; works as proofreader and editor for a tax firm.
1973	Turns down an offer to work as a reporter for CBS; quits proofreading/editing job in Los Angeles.
1974	Wins the Council on Interracial Books for Children Award for *Song of the Trees*.
1975	*Song of the Trees* published by Dial Books.
1975	Moves back to family home in Toledo, Ohio.
1976	Father, Wilbert Lee Taylor, dies. Publishes *Roll of Thunder, Hear My Cry*.
1977	*Roll of Thunder, Hear My Cry* wins the Newbery Medal.
1978	ABC-TV televises *Roll of Thunder, Hear My Cry*, as a three-part miniseries adapted from Taylor's novel.
1981	Publishes *Let the Circle Be Unbroken*.
1985	*Roll of Thunder, Hear My Cry* wins the Buxtehude Bulle Award in West Germany.
1987	Publishes *The Gold Cadillac* and *The Friendship*.
1990	Publishes *The Road to Memphis* and *Mississippi Bridge*.
1995	Publishes *The Well: David's Story*.
1997	Receives the ALAN Award for significant contribution to young adult literature.

1. Mildred D. Taylor: "The Only One"

I was born in a segregated city, in a segregated state, in a segregated America.

—Mildred D. Taylor

The Early Years

Mildred Delois Taylor, called Delois by her immediate family, was born in Jackson, Mississippi, on 13 September 1943, to Wilbert Lee Taylor and Deletha Marie Davis Taylor. Because hospitals were segregated in Mississippi in those days, she was born in their little family home on Everett Street, her mother attended by a local midwife. Taylor was the second and final child of Wilbert and Deletha Taylor. Her older sister, Wilma, had been born about three years earlier. Her father was 24 years old when Taylor was born and worked for a trucking firm in Jackson.[1]

At the time of her birth, the United States was in the middle of World War II. Money and materials were scarce all over the country, but like most families, the Taylors worked hard and made do with what they had. Life for the Taylors, though, and for other blacks living in the southern United States, was made more difficult by the fact that racial segregation severely limited their basic freedoms. Mildred Taylor had just been born, but Wilbert Taylor had lived his entire life in the South, and his family had a long and noble history there. His grandfather, the son of a white Alabama plantation owner and a slave woman, left home in his early teens, made his way to Mississippi, bought land, and built a

1

home there in the late 1800s. Wilbert Taylor's family still owned the land and the home (*SAAS*, 272). Since then, the family had grown into a large, loving, and loyal group who met together often and did whatever they could to support one another.

But even with a large extended family, family land, and family tradition to support him, life in the segregated South remained difficult and often unpleasant for Wilbert Taylor. He loved the South for its beauty and for his roots there, but he hated living in a racist society and worried often about raising his two beautiful daughters in a culture that would consider them inferior because of the color of their skin. Even before Taylor was born, her father had contemplated moving to the North (*SAAS*, 269). He believed that the North offered opportunities for him and his daughters that would never be possible in the segregated South, and he knew his family's lives would be different there, different and, most likely, better. But it's a hard decision to leave your home, family, and history; besides, Wilbert Taylor worked as a trucker, in what was considered a good job for blacks in those days. And now he also had a new daughter to care for.

A few weeks after Taylor's birth, however, the decision to leave the South was essentially made for him. Taylor explains that when she was three weeks old, her father, known for his hot temper, came home from work very angry. He had been involved in a racial incident at work, and he had almost punched a white man. Taylor recalls, "of course, the repercussions could have been terrifying for him and for the rest of us."[2]

Wilbert Taylor was 24 years old and had lived his entire life in the racist society of the South; on that day in October 1943, he decided he had had enough. He left work immediately after the incident, went to the family home on Everett Street, and began to pack his bags (*SAAS*, 268–69). Taylor's family tells the story that as her father put his clothes into his suitcase, his wife unpacked them, all the time wondering what in the world had gotten into her husband, who intended to leave her and her two little children. Later that same day, Taylor's father boarded a train headed north and left behind his family while he looked for a better job and a better life away from Mississippi. Within a week he had

A portrait of the infant Mildred D. Taylor with her older sister, Wilma.

landed a job in a factory in Toledo, Ohio, a job he would keep until his fatal illness in 1976. Two months later, when Taylor was three months old, Wilbert Taylor sent for his family to join him and to begin their new life together in the North. Taylor, with her sister and mother, left Mississippi on a segregated train bound for Ohio (*Booklist*, 740). Just before Christmas in 1943, the Taylors joined the great black migration that took place in the mid-twentieth century, when thousands of southern black families moved North for greater freedom and opportunity. Wilbert Taylor moved his family to Toledo, Ohio, and established what would become a family home for Taylor, her mother, and sister and, at varying times through the coming years, home for many cousins, uncles, and aunts.

A New Life in the North

Upon first arriving in Toledo, the Taylors stayed with friends from Mississippi while Wilbert and Deletha Taylor both worked to save enough money to buy a home of their own. In less than a year, they were able to buy a large duplex on Dorr Street, a busy commercial street in Toledo (the house is described in *The Gold Cadillac*). Though their parents hoped to move to a better location some day, Taylor and Wilma loved it. Taylor recalls that she thought it was a perfect location because, as far as the girls were concerned, everything they might have wanted was on their street or in the nearby neighborhood. Directly across the street from the Taylor home were a fish market and a beauty parlor. Down the street on the corner were a cleaners, a cafe, and a grocery store. Another grocery store and a drug store were at the other end of the block, with a hotel and a bar across the street from them. A block away were more stores, a gas station, and one of the prime attractions of Taylor's youth, the Dixie Theater, where she and her sister saw movies every weekend. Just a block away from her new home was the school, and their church was only three blocks away. An added plus to the convenient location was the neighborly small-town atmosphere where everyone knew everyone else. With all the luxuries and conveniences surrounding this house, Taylor couldn't imagine why her parents would ever consider living anywhere else (*SAAS,* 269).

One reason Wilbert and Deletha Taylor purchased this particular house was because it had plenty of rooms—enough so that, if they needed to, they could accommodate other family members as well. It wasn't long before those extra rooms were put to use.

Taylor's family in 1950. Her father is standing, second from right. Her mother is seated on the arm of the sofa with Taylor sitting next to her.

When World War II ended, two of Taylor's uncles returned from the war, married, and came from the South with their new wives for the opportunities and freedoms to be found in the North. They were welcomed into the Taylor home. Another uncle and aunt soon joined them. They were followed by aunts and first and second cousins from both sides of the family who also came to Toledo seeking freedom and a fresh start. Soon all the rooms in the house were filled, including the coal room in the basement, which had been cleaned out so family could use it. It wasn't unusual for Taylor and Wilma to give up their bedroom to visitors and sleep in the living room or dining room, and the girls never minded at all.

Taylor loved being surrounded by so many family members because it meant there was always someone to talk to. In many ways, her aunts and uncles became surrogate parents, and if her mother or father were busy, she could turn to an aunt or uncle for help or attention. What Taylor remembers as the "good life" was complemented by the presence of many cousins who, for Wilma and Taylor, filled the roles of both playmates and siblings (*SAAS*,

Taylor's family in the kitchen of the house described in *The Gold Cadillac*. Her mother and father are standing at right.

269). The close relationships Taylor developed with her family and extended family early in her childhood have remained with and sustained her throughout her life. Their influence is clear in her writing, where strong and loving families are integral to nearly every story. In her Newbery acceptance speech, Taylor explained, in part, why a strong, extended family played such a key role in *Roll of Thunder, Hear My Cry:* "During my childhood a family that offered aunts and uncles who were second parents, and cousins who were like brothers and sisters, was as natural to me as a mother and father are to most children."[3]

Family Trips to Mississippi

Though Wilbert Taylor left the South, he never let go of his love for *his* South, nor of his loving connection to the family members who remained behind in Mississippi. Throughout his life, he regularly returned with his wife and children to visit his family and roots in the South. He hoped one day to return there permanently. Taylor remembers her father's dream:

> [My father] believed that as the North in the years following the War had held opportunities for Blacks, now the opportunities were in the South and he had, even in his last days, the dream of "going back home." He had never forgotten the feel of the soft red earth. He had never forgotten the goodness of walking on acres of his own land, of knowing that land had a history that stretched back over many generations. There, next to the house which my great-grandfather had built, he hoped to build his own house, surrounding it with flowers and fruit trees, with horses and cows, tending his own land with the love he had felt for it as a boy. ("Newbery," 408)

His children inherited the ambivalence Wilbert Taylor felt for Mississippi. Because of their frequent trips to the South to visit family, Taylor and Wilma fell in love with the beauty of the place, with the memories, and with their family and friends. As they grew older, however, they recognized the segregation and racism that existed in Mississippi in those days, and they learned to fear and hate that situation. But in their early lives, more than almost anything, they loved their frequent trips to Mississippi. These trips remain a fond memory for Taylor, a memory she has described to many audiences as a "twenty-hour picnic." In preparation for these trips, her mother would prepare some of their favorite foods—fried chicken, cake, sweet potato pie—and pack them into a basket along with jugs of ice water and lemonade. Her father would load up their car, placing that basket of goodies on the back seat between Taylor and Wilma, and the two girls could hardly wait until they were out of Toledo to dig into the food. Taylor remembers those trips as wonderful adventures into what seemed like a different world, a different era from what they had left in Toledo ("Newbery," 401).

As wonderful as the travel was, the destination was even better. In her Newbery speech, Taylor reminisced about her childhood days in Mississippi. It was an idyllic time for a young child, playing outside in the warm Mississippi summer sun, by day running barefoot chasing butterflies, by night chasing fireflies. She rode Jack, the mule, and the mare Lady, spent some time picking cotton, and enjoyed the company of cousins and other relatives from her extended family. In the evenings, relatives would gather to visit with one another and to tell stories about friends and relatives they had known. The storytellers, with Taylor's father the best of them all, told lively stories, using gestures, voices, and body movements to enhance their tales. Taylor loved the stories and would sit totally enthralled by what she heard. As she recalled, "It was a magical time" ("Newbery," 401).

The telling of family stories was central to these regular family visits—and to all other Taylor family gatherings. No matter what the event was, the family found time for storytelling, with the adults gathering first, the children joining them when they tired of playing games. The stories mesmerized the children because many times the tales turned into a history of black people that had little in common with the history they learned in school. Family storytellers related incidents about the struggles black people faced in a racist culture, stories that revealed triumph, pride, and tragedy ("Newbery," 404). It was a history that inspired Taylor with pride, hope, and ambition. To this day, she has a vivid recollection of the storytelling sessions:

> I remember my grandparents' house, the house my great-grandfather had built at the turn of the century, and I remember the adults talking about the past. As they talked I began to visualize all the family who had once known the land, and I felt as if I knew them, too. . . .
>
> Many of the stories told were humorous, some were tragic, but all told of the dignity and survival of a people living in a society that allowed them few rights as citizens and treated them as inferiors. Much history was in those stories, and I never tired of hearing them. There were stories about slavery and the days following slavery. There were stories about family and friends.[4]

From these historical accounts, Taylor learned about her great-grandfather, who had been born the son of a white plantation owner in Alabama and a black and Indian slave woman and who eventually left Alabama to buy land and settle in Mississippi. She also learned about her great-grandmother of Indian heritage and about her great-uncles, who were courageous and sometimes hot-headed. She heard stories about other family members and friends and about chain gangs and conflicts with whites. She enjoyed all these stories, but her favorites remained the stories about her father and his siblings growing up on the family home-stead in Mississippi (*Booklist,* 741). It was from these family sto-ries, recounted by many of her relatives, but especially by her father, whom she has described on many occasions as "a master storyteller," that Mildred D. Taylor gained a strong personal sense of family, history, pride, and self. The storytelling tradition had a tremendous impact on the girl and later the woman writer. The oral tradition would influence her own storytelling style, and the stories that she heard at family gatherings became sources for many of her Logan stories.

The stories she heard from her father and extended family members stirred her imagination and also inspired her to become a storyteller herself one day, though it was not until she entered high school that she had a specific idea of what kind of storyteller she wanted to become:

> [My father's] colorful vignettes stirred the romantic in me. I was fascinated by the stories, not only because of what they said or because they were about my family, but because of the man-ner in which my father told them. I began to imagine myself as storyteller, making people laugh at their own human foibles or nod their heads with pride about some stunning feat of heroism. But I was a shy and quiet child, so I turned to creating stories for myself instead, carving elaborate daydreams in my mind.
>
> I do not know how old I was when the daydreams became more than that, and I decided to write them down, but by the time I entered high school, I was confident that I would one day be a writer.[5]

Though the trips to Mississippi remained highlights for Taylor, as she grew older, she became more aware of her surroundings in the South and of the change in her parents when they traveled

Taylor sitting on one of her father's new cars.

south. On their trips into the South, she also observed several incidents that opened her eyes to segregation and racism. In her Newbery Award acceptance speech, she recalls that on one summer trip to Mississippi, she "suddenly felt a climbing nausea as we crossed the Ohio River into Kentucky"(402) and was again reminded by her parents that while they were in the South, they had to stay quiet, let their parents do the talking, and not ask to use the restrooms when they pulled into gas stations. "WHITE ONLY, COLORED NOT ALLOWED" signs on restrooms and drinking fountains, in restaurant and motel windows, reminded her that she was a second-class citizen. It was then that she realized that her mother carried food on the trip not to make it a picnic but because they could not stop at restaurants along the way. She realized that her father pushed through the exhausting 20-hour trip not because he was anxious to get to Mississippi but because they would not be allowed to stay in motels along the way. She realized that they traveled South in family caravans not merely for togetherness but for protection from the police. She saw her father stopped by police on several occasions, not for breaking the law but for being a black man driving a nice car. She even watched him forced to stand spread-eagled against their car while police frisked him. Taylor says that around this time of her life, her family trips to the South began to seem like traveling in a foreign country. Eventually, she came to realize there were two Souths: one of racism that alternately terrified and angered her and one of family and community in which she sensed safety and love and from which she developed a sense of history that made her feel proud of who she was and where she came from (*SAAS*, 270).

Taylor loved being in the rural areas, the land of her family, outside of Jackson, Mississippi. As she recalls, being on the family land was like stepping back into another time because life in the community they were visiting hadn't changed much since the days of her father's childhood: water came from wells, rooms were lit by kerosene lamps and warmed by fireplaces. The homes had no plumbing, electricity, telephones, or televisions. Many of the people still farmed using the old methods and relied on horses and mules as their primary means of transportation (*SAAS*, 270).

The Taylors usually visited the South during holidays, but sometimes the community school where her grandmother taught and where her father had gone as a child would still be open, and she and Wilma would attend classes there. When they visited during the summer, her father would send them into the cotton fields to work with others picking cotton. He wanted his daughters as much as possible to experience his Mississippi world as he had experienced it so they could better understand their parents' lives. He also wanted them to appreciate what was good in the South and at the same time be grateful for the relatively comfortable lives and freedoms they enjoyed in the North. Wilbert Taylor had good reasons for wanting Taylor and Wilma to have these kinds of experiences in the South. Taylor explained that her father told them that unless they understood the lack of freedom for blacks in the South, they could not appreciate the freedom they had in the North. Her father loved Mississippi and told his daughters that because of the family land and history in the South, he felt that if blacks in Mississippi had the same freedoms they had in the North, he would prefer to live in the South (*SAAS* 272).

The Family Storytelling Tradition

Many traditions from the South became a part of the Taylors' lives in Toledo, especially storytelling. But Taylor remembers that books were nearly as much a part of that tradition as story-telling was. In a speech she delivered at the American Booksellers Convention, she recalled a humorous anecdote from 1951 where her book reading got her into some trouble:

> I can't remember when I received the very first book of my own; I just remember I loved it. I remember how proud my parents were that I loved so much to read. I remember as well, however, that I was always getting into trouble for reading all the time. I got into trouble at night when I would sit in the closet when I was supposed to have long been asleep. I got into trouble during the daytime, too, when I would be sitting somewhere hidden, when I was suppose to have been doing my chores. One particular time I got into trouble was during the year I call The Year of the Chicken Pox.
>
> Now, I brought the chicken pox home. There was an epidemic of it going around that year, and I got it at school. I was down sick with it for a while, then my sister got the disease, and my mother had her hands full. But that wasn't the worst of it. Soon my father got it, and my uncles, and several young adult male cousins—they all got it bad, too. The doctor came . . . and he went to all the various rooms and visited all the various patients. One uncle was in such bad shape he was shipped off to the hospital.
>
> Fortunately, however, none of the women got sick. My mother, my aunts, stayed well. I remember thinking, "Aha, it's going to really be great being a woman because women don't get sick." And it's a good thing those women did not get sick because otherwise the house would have fallen into disarray.
>
> Well, since I was the first one to have gotten the disease, I was the first one perky enough to be up and around. The thing was, I couldn't go back to school yet, and with my sister still in bed, I had to find something to do. I decided to read. Now I read

all of my own books several times over, so I went to the book-shelves in the living room. This was a magical place to me because here were stacked all the adult books. Well, I went rummaging through this bookcase, and I found a hardcover volume, and it was really terrific because it had photos in it. The photos were from a movie because the book had been made into a movie. I thought, "Oh, this is going to be great." I took the book and I sat down in my father's favorite chair in the living room, and I pulled the blanket around me and began to read. The title of this book was *Fallen Angel.* Now, I remember this book very well; it was all about a love triangle. It was about a married man having an affair, and it was about murder. I was fascinated. I was eight.

For a couple days my head was buried in that book. I just read and read, and was so comfortable. Now, I didn't understand all the words in *Fallen Angel,* but I understood enough. Since everyone was accustomed to seeing my head buried in a book, no one questioned what I was reading. Besides, as I said, my mother and my aunts had their hands full taking care of all the sick folks, so they paid little attention to my reading. To them I seemed contented, and I certainly was.

But then, as luck would have it, just as I was getting to the really good part, one of my aunts looked over the back of my chair and saw that this was not a picture book in my hands. She said, "Girl, just what are you reading?" I told her, *Fallen Angel.* I wasn't ashamed of it either. My aunt immediately called my mother. "Dee," she said, "look at what this child is reading." My mother looked at the book. "Well, I'm sure she doesn't understand it," she said. "Yes, I do, too," I said.

Now, you know I should've kept my mouth shut, but when you're eight, you want everybody to know how smart you think you are. So I told them all about this book, all about this man and this woman plotting to kill the man's wife. Needless to say, the book was taken away. And that wonderful bookcase in the living room—totally cleared of such fascinating reading. Obviously my mother wasn't intending for a book like *Fallen Angel* to fall into my young hands again. My mother has always watched out for me, and she's still watching out for me today. (*Booklist,* 740)

Taylor's home in Toledo, where she grew up among loving extended family, was a place of happiness and activity. Even after aunts and uncles found their own homes and moved out of the

Taylor's mother, Deletha Marie Davis Taylor.

Taylors' duplex, the family members gathered together often to do things. Her father, uncles, and cousins loved automobiles and would buy the nicest ones they could afford. On summer weekends, they would often caravan to the beach or park where the men would clean and polish their cars while their wives spread out picnic meals and the children played. On other weekends, they would drive to visit family in Detroit, Muncie, Peoria, or Chicago. Sometimes, because Taylor's mother loved baseball, they would drive to Cleveland to watch the Cleveland Indians play. They also took longer trips as a family. In 1953, they visited Buffalo, New York, and Niagara Falls, Canada, and later drove west to California (*SAAS*, 269).

Becoming "the Only One"

Nine years after moving into the duplex on Dorr Street and a few months after their return from their California trip, Wilbert and Deletha Taylor finally moved off that busy commercial street. Taylor's parents retained ownership of the duplex, and relatives moved into the duplex while other family members, Taylor, and her family moved into a large house her parents purchased in a newly integrated Toledo neighborhood. Taylor remembers seeing it for the first time and being stunned by its grandeur, believing it to be as wonderful as the homes she had seen on TV. This house had bedrooms on the second floor, a shower in the bathtub, a breakfast nook, recreation room, three fireplaces, and many windows. At the time, to Taylor, the house seemed so large that she thought she might become lost in it (*SAAS*, 273). In her new home, at least four relatives lived with them for another five years. Her mother still lives in this house.[6]

Moving to a new neighborhood meant changing schools, from the only elementary school she had ever known, one where most of her classmates had been black, to a different school, one where most of the students were white. When Taylor entered fifth grade, she had a few black classmates, but when she started sixth grade in 1954, she was the only black student in her class. That's when she began to feel the pressure of being the "only one" (*SAAS*, 273). Being such an obvious minority made her feel that what she did reflected on her and also on her family and on blacks in general. She believed that because she was "the only one" she could not allow herself to be as good as her classmates, she had to

Eleven-year-old Taylor standing in front of her family's second home in Toledo.

be better. Her drive to excel had little to do with competition; Taylor feared that if she failed, people would say she had failed because she was black. She became more sensitive to being a minority, sometimes thinking that when her classmates laughed at something about her, they were really laughing at her because she was black. Her abhorrence of failure and of being laughed at motivated her to work very hard in her studies, and as a result, she was a good student (*SAAS*, 273–74).

The pressure to excel instilled in Taylor while she was still young the importance of setting goals, of planning ahead. She has said in many places that her father had always told her—and she believed him—that she could do anything she set her mind to, and the ambitions she had while she was young have, as it turned out, directed most of her life. Her longtime friend and editor Phyllis Fogelman wrote that Taylor once said that as she has reflected on her life, she realized that she made all her important decisions while she was still young. The decision to become a writer came when she was 9 or 10 years old. She also wanted to see the world, and at 16 made up her mind she would join the Peace Corps when she graduated from college. Taylor told Fogelman that attending college hadn't really been a decision. Instead, it was something she had always taken for granted because she knew that she would need the four years of study to achieve the goals she had set for herself.[7]

Taylor's experience, and its accompanying pressures in her new elementary school, wasn't the first time she was "the only one," and it wasn't the last. She entered Toledo's Scott High School as a freshman in 1957, and at the time, the school had about a 50-50 balance of white and black students enrolled. But even with 50 percent black enrollment, Taylor still was, in many ways, "the only one." Fogelman says that although high schools in Toledo were integrated city-wide, the schools organized their courses by grouping students by ability levels, a system that handicapped blacks who had attended inferior feeder schools. Because of this arrangement, Taylor was often the only black student in her college preparatory courses, and because she once again found herself "the only one" in her courses, she competed all the harder. It is not too surprising that Taylor had the most success in English. Her classmates knew her as a writer, and in their senior class prophecy in the student yearbook they wrote, "The well-known journalist Mildred Taylor is displaying her Nobel Prize winning novel" (Fogelman, 411). So she remained "the only one," the only black in many of her college-prep courses, the only black senior from her school elected to the National Honor Society, the only student who aspired to—and eventually would—write award-winning novels. "So often," says Taylor, "I felt like the token black. I became accustomed to it, but I never felt comfortable with it. . . . I was always aware that all black people would be reflected in what I did, whether it was good or bad" (*SAAS*, 274).

Fortunately, high school wasn't all tension and work for Taylor. In most ways, she was a typical active, bright high school girl, with many of the usual aspirations of high school girls. About those days, she says, "I'm afraid I was one of those students who was a class officer, an editor of the school newspaper, and a member of the honor society, when what I really wanted to be was a cheerleader. I remember how disappointed I was when I failed to make the cheerleading squad and my father telling me that I had greater things cut out for me. Believe me, that wasn't much consolation then!" (Fogelman, 411–12). Her father was right, of course; there were many great things in store for her—two academic degrees, two years of service in the Peace Corps, travel, various jobs, and eventually a career as one of America's most successful and best-known writers of books for young readers.

College and the Peace Corps

Taylor graduated from Scott High School in 1961 and the next fall enrolled at the University of Toledo. Even though she still had dreams of becoming a writer, her parents convinced her to major in something more practical than creative writing or journalism. They knew that very few people could make a living as a creative writer, and they knew of no black journalists in any of the local media. Taylor's parents encouraged her to get a degree in teaching, a field in which they were confident she could one day get a job. So Taylor enrolled in the school of education with a major in English and a minor in history, taking as many creative writing courses as possible along the way. Mixed with her dreams of writing were dreams of travel, and throughout her college years, Taylor looked ahead to one day working in the Peace Corps.

From her youth, Taylor had always dreamed of traveling to exotic places around the world, but for many years she was never sure how she would manage such travel. In 1960 she attended a brief speech by John F. Kennedy and found her answer: she would serve in the Peace Corps. As an African American, Taylor had long had an interest in Africa, especially in Ethiopia. She was attracted by the country's geography, culture, and history (Ethiopia is one of the few African countries not colonized by Europeans), and she admired Emperor Haile Selassie. She made up her mind that if she had a chance to get into the Peace Corps, she would do whatever she could to be assigned to Ethiopia. While still in high school, she began to count down the days until she would go to Africa (*SAAS* 277). Her family knew of her aspirations, and sometimes she endured some teasing from cousins and other family members about her Peace Corps dream, but the family really didn't take her dream seriously. They believed she would grow out of it. Throughout her years in college, she received information from the Peace Corps and continued to study about the program and Ethiopia in preparation for her eventual application. In her junior year she completed the lengthy application process of essays, tests, and interviews, then waited for a response. Still, no one in her family believed she'd really go.

During her senior year in college, Taylor had to spend an entire day taking a series of written examinations as a final part of her Peace Corps application. Taylor's father took her to the testing site and met her outside after she completed the exams. She was exhausted and discouraged. "I don't think I passed," she told her father. Still believing that she wouldn't go if accepted, he replied, "I'm sure you did well."

Despite his encouragement after her exam, Taylor's father was adamantly opposed to her serving in the Peace Corps. He felt she was too young; Africa was too far away; it was all too dangerous, and she would have no protection. Her uncles also discouraged her from going. They lived in the racist South and had served in the segregated armed forces during World War II; they felt that given the treatment blacks received from America, blacks should feel no particular call to serve America. Men in the family had traveled overseas for the military, but no women in the family had ever been overseas. Taylor's mother wasn't happy about the possibility of her daughter spending two years in Africa, but resigned herself to the idea. Only Taylor's sister, Wilma, seemed to think it would be a great adventure. None of this affected Taylor, however. She would not change her mind; she was going to Ethiopia (*SAAS*, 279).

Taylor was ecstatic when she received her invitation to join the Peace Corps, and it was only then that her family, especially her father, realized that she really was going to go to Africa. During the Christmas break of her senior year, her father told her, "No. No way are you going." Taylor replied, "I'm twenty-one now; I can go," and the battle of wills was on. Hoping to change her mind, Taylor's father took her to Mississippi over the Easter holiday so she could talk to her grandparents about her Peace Corps plans. He was certain they would talk her out of leaving the country. To his great surprise—and disappointment—instead of discouraging her, Taylor's grandmother encouraged her to go. "I think it a wonderful opportunity," she told Taylor.

Still, her father refused to back down and even began doing everything he could to keep her from going. In order to serve abroad, Taylor was required to have a physical examination, but the nearest Peace Corps medical facility was in Michigan. Hoping to finally undo her Peace Corps dream, her father refused to loan her a car for the trip and refused to drive her there himself. Taylor finally arranged to have the physical done locally. She says that when her father realized he couldn't undermine the admissions process, he tried to bribe her a little. "If you don't go, if you stay," he told her, "I'll buy you a brand new car. It'll be your graduation present." But even the lure of a new car couldn't sway Taylor, and she and her father remained at loggerheads over the issue.

The Taylors were a faithful, prayerful family; consequently, Taylor and her mother prayed often for help in resolving the Peace Corps conflict between Taylor and her father. One night her father returned home from the church where he served as a deacon and announced, "Something like a miracle happened in church tonight." A young African man had spoken at the church that evening; he told of the great, positive influence American missionaries had had on him, helping him get an education and eventually come to the United States, where he was currently a medical student. His story changed Wilbert Taylor's attitude about the Peace Corps almost immediately. "God meant for you to do this," he told Taylor that night, and from that moment, he did everything he could to help her prepare for her Peace Corps work.

In 1965, Taylor graduated from the University of Toledo with a bachelor's degree in education. A week after graduation, she attended a Peace Corps training camp at the University of Utah, which was followed by three weeks of training on the Navajo Indian reservation near Tuba City, Arizona. By September she was in Yirga 'Alem, Ethiopia, ready to teach English and history.

Fogelman wrote that Mildred D. Taylor recalled her two years in Ethiopia as the happiest in her life. Taylor "fell in love with Africa—the variety of landscape, the sound of singing in the fields, the people who accepted and cared for her—and she has always hoped to return. Taylor considered her years in Africa as the happiest period of her adult life; she admired the people, their culture and history. As the end of her stay in Ethiopia approached, Mildred had terrible nightmares about having to leave, only to awaken each morning filled with joy that she was still there" (Fogelman, 412). Though her Peace Corps training had prepared her to expect some prejudice from the Ethiopians, Taylor discovered instead that she was the first black American most of the people from the mountain village had met, and she was accepted by them as a long-lost daughter, a descendant of the people who had been forced into slavery hundreds of years earlier. The village people who came to know her used family terms to address her: mother, sister, daughter (*SAAS*, 280). The longer she stayed in Ethiopia, the more Taylor grew to love the country and its people. Taylor says that in many ways Ethiopia reminded her of her South—the roads, the heritage, the fields, cohesive families, the singing, and the storytelling. Removed from the racism of the United States, she felt good about herself, and she admired the solid sense of identity of the Ethiopians and the pride they had in themselves. For a time she considered staying in Africa permanently, but in the end she knew she must return to her home and family in America.

Taylor returned to the United States in the summer of 1967. For the next eight months, she worked as a Peace Corps recruiter stationed in Chicago but traveling throughout the Midwest on college recruiting jobs. She then spent three months working as an instructor in a Peace Corps training camp in Maine. In September

1968 at the end of her first year back in the United States, she moved to Boulder, Colorado, where she enrolled in the journalism graduate program at the University of Colorado (*SAAS*, 280).

In her first months of graduate study, Taylor was invited to attend a meeting of the Black Student Alliance. She did and soon became quite involved with the organization and some of its allied groups, the Black Studies Program and the Black Education Program. In what Taylor calls "a necessary period" (*SAAS*, 281), she worked with other black students at the university to develop black pride and to improve conditions and opportunities for blacks across campus. Taylor played an important role in redefining the Black Studies Program, and after she received her master of arts degree in August 1969, she developed a study skills and tutorial program for the Black Studies Program and started work as study skills coordinator at the university (*SAAS*, 281).

The Beginnings of a Writing Career

A few months after she graduated, a visiting editor from *Life* magazine who had read an article Taylor had written about Black Studies met with her and invited her to write an article about the Black Studies movement and its impact at the University of Colorado. Taylor was ecstatic about this big opportunity and immediately began working on the article. After she had finished her draft, she allowed members of the Black Student Alliance to edit the article before she sent it on to *Life*. In what would become a turning point in her career, the article was rejected because the writing was too weak and lacked the vitality the *Life* editor had seen in Taylor's original article. The rejection was a bitter disappointment for Taylor, but she turned it into an important learning experience. In the rejection letter, the *Life* editor urged Taylor to be true to herself as a writer; Taylor knew the editor was right and realized she had failed herself as a writer by letting her work be diluted by others. Losing the opportunity to be published in *Life* magazine caused Taylor to reflect on her own goals and values, and in the summer of 1970, she returned to Ethiopia to reconsider her goals. In the fall she returned to her job in the Black Studies program where she worked for nine months before leaving Colorado for California (*SAAS*, 282).

Taylor settled in Los Angeles in 1971 to pursue her dream of becoming a writer. Initially she tried writing and living on her savings, but when her savings ran low, she found a job as a temporary office worker. The work was undemanding, and it allowed Taylor time for herself and plenty of physical and creative energy for writing (*SAAS*, 282). She continued to write in the evenings and on weekends, completing many stories and sending them off, hoping to break into print somewhere. A year later, after many stories and many rejections, Taylor grew discouraged and began considering other career paths that would allow her to use her experience and education. Perhaps with the hope of settling down or refocusing her life, in August of 1972 Taylor married Errol Zea-Daly, a Central American man she had met shortly after she had arrived in Los Angeles (unfortunately, the marriage wouldn't last; the couple divorced three years later). Not long after her marriage, she was offered a job as a reporter for CBS but after serious consideration turned it down. "Despite the despair from all the rejections from all the publishing houses I had sent my work," she explains, "somehow I knew that my future as a writer lay not in journalism, but in books" (*SAAS*, 283).

Taylor's career-making break came in October 1973, when she entered a contest for minority writers sponsored by the Council on Interracial Books for Children. She selected her story about a tree-cutting incident on the family land in Mississippi and submitted the manuscript on the day of deadline. In February 1974 she received news that she had won the Afro-American category of the contest. The award led to a book contract with Dial Books, who published Taylor's contest-winning manuscript as *Song of the Trees* in the spring of 1975, and the path of Taylor's writing career was set: all of her books since then have been based on family stories, and all have been published by Dial. The dream of her youth has been realized.

Just one year later, using the lessons she learned from revising *Song of the Trees,* Taylor completed *Roll of Thunder, Hear My Cry,* which would win the 1977 Newbery Medal and become her best-known book. The American Library Association's Newbery Medal has been awarded annually since 1922 to an American author of the most outstanding book for children in the prior year. It is the most prestigious and coveted award for young adult writers, one most authors can only dream of winning. Taylor, however, recalls that winning the Newbery was not a surprise. "I know that sounds vain," she says, but by the time she had completed the novel, she had a feeling it would win. "I was inspired by the song 'Roll of Thunder,' which came to me when I was most troubled about my book. At the moment the song came to me I knew the book would win the Newbery Award, and I told my father so." Her editors had told her that *Roll of Thunder* was among those being given final consideration for the award and that if it did win, she would receive a call on a particular Monday night. She still recalls that January evening. Her mother was working the night shift at the local hospital, and Taylor was alone at her family home in Toledo waiting for the call. She kept waiting and waiting, until sometime after ten o'clock the call came; she had won the 1977 Newbery Medal. Taylor was ecstatic, of course, and immediately called her mother at work to tell her the news, then called all the family. The award established her as a leading writer for young people and allowed her to continue her dream of writing full-time, the only career she has had since that time.

Many of the keys to Taylor's success can be traced directly to her youth: the steady influence of her wise and loving father; the understanding and unconditional support of her mother; the family trips to Mississippi; living with a loving, loyal family; discovering racism; being "the only one" in school. The challenges she faced—and overcame with the gentle support of her father, mother, and other family members—gave her the strength and experience to accomplish some of her most satisfying professional work: telling the stories of the Logan family of Mississippi. In many ways, her protagonist, Cassie Logan, is also "the only one."

She's the only daughter in her family, the only child to witness a number of terrible events, the only one in her school whose family is made up of educated landowners, the only one with the courage to face up to racism and discrimination. Many of the lessons Taylor learned, Cassie also learns, and the challenges they both have faced have shaped them into memorable, admirable characters.

2. Becoming a Writer: A Family's—and Father's—Influence

. . . a legacy which has enriched me all of my life.

—Mildred D. Taylor

Foundation of Family

In an article about Mildred D. Taylor in *Language Arts* in 1981, Sharon Dussel concluded, "The influence a strong, supporting family can have on a child's development is most definitely seen in the life and work of Mildred D. Taylor."[1] Others before and after Dussel have come to similar conclusions about the powerful effect family has had on Taylor and her writing. Mildred D. Taylor herself makes no secret of this influence. In her Newbery Award acceptance speech she avowed that anyone reading *Roll of Thunder, Hear My Cry* would find plenty of evidence of strong family ties and the effects of her father and her family's teachings ("Newbery," 402). Even before her stories unfold on page one, in every book she acknowledges the contributions her family has made to her stories and to her life. In her first book, *Song of the Trees,* the dedication nods to several family members: her mother, "the quiet, lovely one, who urged perseverance"; her father, "the strong, steadfast one, who wove the tales of history"; her sister Wilma, "the beautiful, laughing one, who lifted my spirits high"; her grandparents "Mrs. Lee Annie Bryant, Mr. Hugh Taylor, and Mrs. Lou Emma Taylor, the wise ones, who bridged the generations between slavery and freedom"; and to her family "who fought and survived." In the books that followed, she made clear her family's influence on her writing. *Roll of Thunder, Let the Circle Be Unbroken, The Friendship, Road to Memphis,* and *Mississippi Bridge* are all dedicated to her father. Three of those books have identical or nearly identical dedications: "To the memory of my beloved father who lived many adventures of the boy Stacey and who was in essence the man David." *Road to Memphis* is also dedicated to her uncle, James Taylor, who she says, "has always been like a second father." *The Gold Cadillac* is dedicated to her mother. *The Well* is once again dedicated to her father, but also to her mother, sister, daughter, and her entire family, past and present.

Her fierce—and literal—dedication to family goes beyond the front matter of her books. In her speeches and writing, she consistently acknowledges the influence of family, particularly her father, in all her writing. Those few who know Mildred D. Taylor personally and the many who have read her books soon come to envy the loving, close-knit real Taylor family and the fictional Logans. Regina Hayes, one of Taylor's first editors at Dial, said that after getting to know Taylor, it's difficult not to wish that you could be included in her family. One public example of Taylor's love for and loyalty to family was the Newbery Award banquet. Initially, she was told by Phyllis Fogelman that she could have two guests at the awards ceremony, but Taylor said she'd need to have more than two. After trimming her guest list down to the bare minimum, she told Fogelman by mail that she'd like 30 invitations for family members to attend the banquet. All 30 attended. For her, the family gathering at the Newbery Award ceremony was symbolic of the gatherings of her childhood when her family came together often to play, celebrate, and perhaps most importantly, tell stories of their present and past ("Newbery," 403–4).

Taylor at the Newbery Award ceremony with her Aunt Curtis and Uncle James Taylor.

Storytelling Tradition

Perhaps some of Taylor's fondest, if not the most powerful, memories of her childhood are connected to family gatherings and the storytelling sessions that naturally grew out of them. Some of these get-togethers took place at her parents' home in Toledo, but she has especially vivid memories of those that happened on Taylor land in Mississippi. In her acceptance speech for the *Boston Globe/Horn Book* Award, she talked about her memories of her grandparents' house, the house her great-grandfather built in the early 1900s; she also remembered that her adult relatives told stories about Taylor ancestors. "As they talked I began to visualize all the family who had once known the land, and I felt as if I knew them, too. I met them all through the stories told, stories told with such gusto and acting skills that people long since dead lived again through the voices and movements of the storytellers" (*Boston Globe*, 179–80). At the time she sat enthralled by her family's tales, Taylor did not realize that one day the people telling the stories, the people in the stories, and some of the stories themselves would become the foundation for her own stories.

The storytelling tradition passed from her father and other relatives to her, instilling in Taylor the desire—and the skills—to tell stories herself, stories based upon her own family's experiences and history. She says that her dream of one day becoming a writer had its roots in her family's storytelling tradition. Taylor told Phyllis Fogelman that she made the decision to be a writer when she was nine or ten years old and that as a writer she wanted to show strong individuals in loving families, the same kinds of individuals and families that surrounded her as she grew up. She also felt the need, she says, to portray the beauty, romance, love, and the sense of pride she learned from her family, to show blacks as heroic, and to present such a vivid representation of her world that readers would feel they had become a part of it (*SAAS*, 277). These goals were ambitious for a young writer, and early in her career her inability to meet her own high standards frustrated her considerably.

Learning about Writing

Despite her dream and the storytelling talent inspired by and inherited from her family, writing didn't come easily to Taylor. She once confessed to her editor that she never really liked writing and felt she wasn't all that good at it. "But once I had made up my mind, I had no doubts about doing it. It was just something that would happen someday" (Fogelman, 410). By the time she entered high school, her own awareness of her determination and writing skills, and the lesson her father had taught since her early childhood that she could do anything she set her mind to, gave her the confidence that she would become a writer. Along with that confidence, she had a sure idea that she desperately wanted her writing to present a more accurate picture of blacks, to demonstrate their perseverance, to show that black families have strong fathers and mothers. She wanted to write about unified families with happy children who were loved by their parents, children that her readers would admire and identify with ("Newbery," 405).

Her determination to write and her clear vision of what she would write were necessary because her early work often disappointed her; her reflections on her writing struggles reveal the insecurity that plagues many young writers. For a time, Taylor wondered if she would ever have the talent to write as well as she wanted to. As a high school student, she often questioned her own abilities, especially when she compared herself to the white students in her English classes for whom, it seemed, writing came easily. Those students often were called upon to read their papers aloud as models of good writing; Taylor too was sometimes called on to read her papers aloud in class, but one of her clearest memories of high school is the day her teacher read one of her stories out loud as an example of poor writing (*SAAS*, 277).

Rather than be discouraged by what she perceived as failure, Taylor continued to write, working diligently to improve her skills, but in her efforts to become a great writer, to write like the authors she studied in school, she forgot for a time what she wanted to write about. Once again, the effects of her family and their stories helped her find her way. One day she decided to try to write some of the heroic family stories she had heard over the years; one of the first such stories she tried would many years later become a book, *The Friendship*. Taylor felt comfortable using family stories as the foundation, but writing even these familiar tales was difficult. "In the beginning I didn't have the power to put the story on paper. For me the story had to be as powerful on paper as it had been when I had heard it told by the storytellers. I wanted the reader to feel what I had felt" (*Boston Globe*, 181). Though she had finally discovered what should be the content of her stories, she still hadn't discovered the right voice and style. Fortunately, she soon would.

The confidence inspired by her father and the encouragement of another high school teacher helped prevent Taylor from giving up on her dream. A teacher who had read one of her stories liked it and encouraged her to submit it to a citywide writing contest. The story didn't even place in the contest, but it did play a pivotal role in the evolution of Taylor's writing because she had written about a family incident and for the first time used the first-person point of view. The new perspective added verve to her writing that had previously been lacking. Her teacher noticed the difference and encouraged Taylor to continue with it. This experience helped her discover that by using first-person narration, she was recasting her stories in a style similar to the language of her family storytellers (*SAAS*, 277).

The use of first-person narration had eluded Taylor during her younger years because as a student in the 1950s, taught a literature curriculum dominated by classic white authors, she didn't recognize that the storytelling tradition could be a model for her own writing. Instead, she aspired to write like the great authors she studied in school, Ernest Hemingway, John Steinbeck, Jane Austen, and Charles Dickens, because she believed that great literature could only be written in styles similar to those employed by great writers. Her attempts to pattern her work after the literary masters left her writing "sounding stiff and unconvincing. It was an unnatural style for me. I could write well enough, but I could not convey what I wanted to convey with this style" (*SAAS*, 277). With that important lesson in mind, Taylor continued to write in high school and through college. Dreaming of success, she entered many writing contests, cranking out stories longhand and feeding the manuscript pages to her sister, Wilma, who typed them without revision. Unfortunately, Taylor never won any of those contests, in part, she says, because she hadn't yet learned the importance of revision.

At 19 Taylor completed her first novel, *Dark People, Dark World*. It was a story, told in first person, of a young, blind white man who, to escape his own unhappy world, fled to the black ghetto of Chicago. She submitted the manuscript to a publisher in New York under the male pen name "M. D. Taylor" and actually heard back from an editor who reported that he was interested in her book but felt it was too long. He recommended that she shorten the novel and resubmit it as a novella; Taylor rejected his suggestions because as an inexperienced writer, she had no way of knowing how scarce such letters of encouragement are. In addition, she recalls that she "was very naive and full of artistic self-righteousness. I felt the manuscript was too great to cut. So I didn't cut it. Instead, I put it in a drawer and left it there. That was probably the wisest thing I could have done. I had a lot to learn" (*SAAS*, 278). The novel has never been published.

Finding and Relying on Family Support

The influence and importance of family continued after high school. At the University of Toledo, though she took as many creative writing courses as she could, she majored in English education rather than writing because her parents wanted her to have a practical degree. During her Peace Corps service in Ethiopia, she felt comfortable because the people with whom she worked embraced her as family. When she enrolled in graduate school at the University of Colorado, far away from home and family, she did what she had done in Ethiopia: she found a surrogate family among those around her. She became active in the Black Student Association there, making many friends and being very involved in their work, and the close association with BSA members provided the familiar, almost familial, support she thrived on. Perhaps because of the absence of the close family she had become so accustomed to, Taylor began to question the direction her life had taken. In the summer of 1970, she returned to Ethiopia to reconsider her career goals, then returned to Colorado in the fall to work in the Black Education Program for nine months before leaving the university to go to California to pursue her goal of becoming a writer.

In Los Angeles, Taylor wrote steadily and in relative isolation for more than a year but never had anything published. It wasn't long before she became frustrated with her lack of writing success, but the faith instilled in her by her parents sustained her.

Her mother's quiet support combined with her father's constant reminders from her youth that she could accomplish anything she set her mind to gave her confidence that if she worked at writing long enough, she would eventually be able to tell her stories with the right "bright spark of life in words" that the stories deserved. But even with the confidence inspired by her parents, she grew impatient, wondering if her stories would ever have the vitality of the world that inspired them ("Newbery," 405). Throughout those years, however, Taylor continued to write and eventually rediscovered the power her family and their stories offered to her as a writer.

The isolated writing life, she realized, was not for her. "Writing alone made me too weak emotionally; I needed an outside social force, something in which I could also be creative but which would be people-oriented in a different way" (Fogelman, 413). For a time, she considered various other careers—a reporter for CBS, editor/proofreader, international trainer—but none of those seemed right for her. She realized that she would be happiest writing books (*SAAS*, 283).

The Big Break

The books that held her future were books about her own family, told in the same storytelling style she had grown up with. In the fall of 1973, Taylor heard about a writing contest sponsored by the Council on Interracial Books for Children just days before the deadline. Three days before the manuscript was due, she began searching through her stacks of rejected stories looking for something suitable for the contest. One of the stories she considered was a story her father had told about a family incident from the 1930s when some trees on the family land in Mississippi were cut down. She had tried writing the story in third person from a boy's point of view and later from a grandmother's point of view, but neither version had worked. On reading both versions of the story, she realized that this story was the one she wanted to use for the contest, but she wasn't sure how to revise it.

On that weekend in October, with deadline pressure mounting, the years she had spent listening to family storytellers, the years of study, the frustrating years of writing without success finally paid off. As Taylor worked on rewriting her story, her narrator came out of nowhere: Cassie Logan, storyteller. It was immediately clear to Taylor that the story of spunky, proud Cassie had to be told in the storytelling tradition that was Taylor's own heritage: first person. All through the weekend, Taylor wrote and revised the story of the cutting of the trees, finishing it early Monday morning. Friends at work helped her to edit and retyped the final manuscript, and with their help, she met the midnight contest deadline (*SAAS,* 283). That manuscript, *Song of the Trees,* won the contest and launched Taylor's writing career. Since the publication of that book in 1975, in the seven books that have followed, Taylor has never deviated from the tradition of using first-person narration to tell stories from her own family and their history. Interestingly, her father the storyteller was a little surprised that Taylor integrated so much from family stories into her books. After reading *Song of the Trees* and a draft of *Roll of Thunder,* he remarked, "I never realized you were paying such attention."

Winning the Council on Interracial Books for Children contest gave Taylor the chance to meet several New York publishers to discuss publication of her winning manuscript and to fulfill a childhood dream of hers: to one day meet with a publisher and sign her first book contract. She had met with a few other publishers before coming to Dial Books, where she met Phyllis Fogelman and Regina Hayes. Hayes recalls their first meeting fondly, saying that, "Mildred essentially interviewed us." Fogelman said that they liked Taylor immediately. "We were immensely impressed with her dignity and self-possession and with her seriousness and sense of responsibility to herself as a writer. She not only was willing to make revisions, she welcomed any suggestions she felt would improve her book" (Fogelman, 413).

The feeling was mutual. Taylor decided to sign with Dial Books, a decision she said was the best thing she could have done. She liked Fogelman and Hayes, and she appreciated their direct and honest approach to her writing. Taylor wanted to publish her work in its very best condition, and she knew that Dial would insist on high-quality writing from her. That made her decision to sign with them easy (*SAAS*, 283–84). By signing with Dial, Taylor once again found a way to create a family niche that would sustain her. In essence, she extended her family to include Fogelman and Hayes, two talented editors who soon became two valuable friends. Her Dial publishing family has provided her the stability and care she always enjoyed at home with her relatives in Toledo and Mississippi, and the relationship has been mutually beneficial. Taylor has remained loyal to Dial, which has published all of her books, including *Roll of Thunder, Hear My Cry,* which became one of their all-time best-selling novels for young adults.

Establishing Her Writer's Niche

On her way back to Los Angeles after signing with Dial in New York, Taylor stopped off in Toledo to spend a few days with her family. One morning her father and her uncle James Taylor (the one upon which Little Man is based) were talking about the family story from which Taylor had drawn *Song of the Trees.* That story led to another story, one she hadn't heard before. It was about a black boy who started hanging around with two white boys and how the three of them had broken into a store and killed the storekeeper; the black boy was blamed for the murder. As Taylor listened to it, she knew that story would become the basis for her second book. Taylor successfully combined that story with elements of her family and their stories into a novel, *Roll of Thunder, Hear My Cry,* that in 1977 would win the American Library Association's highest honor for a single book, the Newbery Medal.

In writing *Song of the Trees, Roll of Thunder, Hear My Cry,* and the later books in the Logan family saga, Taylor consistently drew upon the family, friends, and stories she had known all her life. She patterned Stacey Logan, the oldest of the Logan children, after her own father; Christopher-John and Little Man Logan,

Taylor as a young girl with her Aunt Sadie. Much of Cassie Logan's physical description is based on this aunt.

Stacey's younger brothers, were based on two of Taylor's uncles; the narrator, Cassie Logan, Taylor drew from the character of one of her aunts and her sister Wilma, and to some degree, herself; hot-tempered Uncle Hammer is patterned after two legendary great-uncles who had shown great courage growing up in Mississippi. The children's mother, Mary Logan, a straightforward and hardworking mother and teacher, was based on Taylor's grandmother, who had also been a teacher in Mississippi. David Logan, the children's father, came from Taylor's father and grandfather who had, as David had, worked on the railroad during the Depression. Taylor used other material from her family stories to develop her Logan family saga:

> I drew much of the [Logan] family's history from the history of my own family, from the history of the young man, born his father's slave, who had acquired land in a community where most black people and many white people sharecropped or were tenants. I drew the characters of the many people who populate the Logan books from people I had met year after year whenever the family went south. They were people who lived in Jackson or in my father's or my mother's rural community. The land, the house, the school, the history are all drawn from that community of lives as I remember them back then, and as I remember the stories told. (*SAAS*, 284)

In examining Taylor's use of family history in her books, Mary Turner Harper concluded that the contents of Taylor's books are generated in much the same way that Alex Hailey created material for *Roots* with "faction," a blend of fact and fiction. By combining stories recalled from her childhood with historical fact, Taylor presents "a fiction that is functional—one that enables young readers to experience a world sometimes alien to them but, at the same time, one that allows them to establish a kinship with characters in their own age group who must confront the challenges of growing up in a less than ideal world."[2]

Phyllis Fogelman and Regina Hayes were pleased with the success of *Song of the Trees,* and they both felt that Taylor had a bright career ahead of her. As with all new writers, however, they weren't sure what to expect of her next book. Hayes recalls that when the editors read the manuscript of *Roll of Thunder,* they were stunned by its beauty and power. As good as *Song of the Trees* had been, it still hadn't prepared them for the quality and scope of Taylor's second book. In her *Horn Book* article, Fogelman reflected on their reaction to the manuscript and how it showcased Taylor's writing ability:

> Her growth as a writer has been extraordinary and wonderfully exciting for us [Fogelman and Regina Hayes]. Every small bit of editorial guidance offered was eagerly received and acted upon. When revisions of *Roll of Thunder, Hear My Cry* were complete, all of us who read the manuscript were struck by the dramatic way in which Mildred's talent had come to fruition. Her power as a writer was astonishing even to us. In retrospect, one can see how the first book was the seed, the preparation for the second, but at the time we marveled at her growth. The ability to grow so remarkably attests once again to Mildred's determination and discipline. (Fogelman, 413)

In Taylor's Newbery Award acceptance speech, she gives credit for her determination and discipline to her family and especially to her father, who had died just months before she received news of the Newbery Award.

Wilbert Taylor's Influence

Shortly after her father's death, Taylor wrote her author's note to *Roll of Thunder,* a tribute to the influence of her family on her life and her writing. Taylor acknowledged her father, the storyteller, "for without his words my words would not have been." She also expressed gratitude to her ancestors who made the history and to her family storytellers who preserved that history from generation to generation, keeping it alive until Taylor herself could weave her family tales into stories of her own that she could share with millions of readers all over the world. From those stories, Taylor learned self-respect and family pride, something she could not have learned anywhere else. Her family's traditions and stories helped her understand her family heritage and gain a stronger personal identity (*SAAS*, 285).

Taylor most often credits her father for instilling in her the stories and values that fill her books. She has described her father as a kind man, one who worked hard, loved and cared for his family, and shared with them the wisdom and insight of his own experience. But he was also very strong willed and set in his ways. Though he was reasonable, it was difficult to get him to change his mind once he had made a decision. He also had a quick temper, much like that of Uncle Hammer in the Logan stories. In her author's note to *Roll of Thunder, Hear My Cry*, Taylor described her father and what he had taught her:

> From my father the man I learned even more, for he was endowed with a special grace that made him tower above other men. He was warm and steadfast, a man whose principles would not bend, and he had within him a rare strength that sustained not only my sister and me and all the family but all those who sought his advice and leaned upon his wisdom.
>
> He was a complex person, yet he taught me many simple things, things important for a child to know: how to ride a horse and how to skate; how to blow soap bubbles and how to tie a kite knot that met the challenge of the March winds; how to bathe a huge faithful mongrel dog named Tiny. In time, he taught me complex things too. He taught me of myself, of life. He taught me of hopes and dreams. And he taught me the love of words. Without his teachings, without his words, my words would not have been.[3]

Taylor describes her father as a special man with strong faith in himself, a man who, despite the racism and prejudice of the world in which he lived, suffered no sense of inferiority. Though he lacked the formal education Taylor herself was fortunate enough to receive, he "tempered [her] learning with his wisdom." Taylor considered her father a master storyteller, but in her Newbery Award acceptance speech, she acknowledges that he was much more than that: "A highly principled, complex man who did not have an excellent education or a white-collar job, he had instead strong moral fiber and a great wealth of what he always said was simply plain common sense" ("Newbery," 402). In addition to being the head of Taylor's immediate family, her father was also recognized as the head of the extended family and often mediated disputes among family members. He was respected and looked up to by members of his and his wife's families. Her father also instilled in Taylor a love of stories and books, a strong sense of self-worth, and a deep appreciation for the importance of family. His confidence in her sustained her through the dark days when she would spend hours and hours writing only to have her stories rejected one after another. Phyllis Fogelman saw firsthand the effects Wilbert Taylor had on his daughter:

> Mildred often speaks of her father as a determining factor in her life, the person who more than anyone else gave her a sense of worth and conviction, and this was particularly true during the years when she was becoming aware of the different directions her life might take. He taught her that all possibilities were open to her if she made up her mind that she could accomplish what she wanted. (Fogelman, 412)

Taylor's mother has had an equally powerful influence on her. Wilbert Taylor taught Taylor important lessons of life and passed on the storytelling tradition, but Deletha Taylor provided the quiet and consistent support that has been vital to Taylor throughout her life. When Taylor and her father were battling over the Peace Corps, her mother supported her. When Taylor's father died, her mother filled the void left in Taylor's life. When Taylor faced rocky financial times later in her career, her mother was there to help. Taylor says that her mother's influence, though in many ways different from her father's influence, has been every bit as important in her life and her writing career.

Without that kind of sustaining confidence, Taylor might easily have given up writing and pursued a career as a TV journalist, an international trainer, or a teacher. Whenever she doubted her abilities, her mother encouraged her and she recalled what her father had always taught her and her sister: "that we were somebody, that we were important and could do or be anything we set our minds to do or be. He was not the kind of father who demanded As on report cards, although he was pleased when we got them, or ranted and raved if there was a D or two. He was more concerned about how we carried ourselves, how we respected ourselves and others, and how we pursued the principles upon which he hoped we would build our lives" ("Newbery,"

402). Those same principles that Wilbert Taylor impressed on his daughters found their way into the characters of David Logan and his children. In *Let the Circle Be Unbroken,* Stacey Logan says to his friend Moe something that could have come directly from the lips of Wilbert Taylor: "Papa says you can do jus' 'bout anything you set your mind to do, you work hard enough."[4]

Wilbert Taylor took all the time necessary to help his daughters learn and grow. It was time well spent, especially in light of the fact that his black daughters were growing up in a society dominated by whites, a society that was often cruel and discriminatory. As Taylor recalled in her Newbery speech, her father's lessons helped prepare her and Wilma for life outside the comfortable, safe, and insular environment of their home and family:

> There was never a moment when he was too busy or too tired to share my problems or to give guidance to my sister and me. Through him my growing awareness of a discriminatory society was accompanied by a wisdom that taught me that anger in itself was futile, that to fight discrimination I needed a stronger weapon. When my family was refused seating in a Wyoming restaurant, he taught me that I must gain the skill to destroy such bigotry; when "For Sale" signs forested the previously all-white neighborhood into which we had moved, he taught me pride in our new home as well as in myself by reminding me that how I saw myself was more important than how others saw me; and when I came home from school one day versed in propaganda against the Soviet Union, he softly reminded me that Black people in the United States of the fifties had no more rights than I had been told the citizens of the Soviet Union had. From that I learned to question, to reason. ("Newbery," 402–3)

In addition to teaching her the lessons of life, Taylor's father also taught her stories and how to tell them.

> He could tell a fine old story that made me hold my sides with rolling laughter and sent happy tears down my cheeks, or a story of stark reality that made me shiver and be grateful for my own warm, secure surroundings. He could tell stories of beauty and grace, stories of gentle dreams, and paint them as vividly as any picture with splashes of character and dialogue. His mem-

ory detailed every event of ten or forty years or more before, just as if it had happened yesterday.

By the fireside in our northern home or in the South where I was born, I learned a history not then written in books but one passed from generation to generation on the steps of moonlit porches and beside dying fires in one-room houses, a history of great-grandparents and of slavery and of the days following slavery; of those who lived still not free, yet who would not let their spirits be enslaved. From my father the storyteller I learned to respect the past, to respect my own heritage and myself. (author's note, *Roll of Thunder*)

That heritage of her family and their experiences in Mississippi eventually became the foundation for all of her books.

Relying on Family Stories

Taylor has said many times that David Logan and Stacey Logan are patterned after her own father, and the parallels between David Logan and Wilbert Taylor are abundant in her books. In *Roll of Thunder* and *Let the Circle Be Unbroken,* Papa Logan often talks to Cassie about the importance of family, reinforcing some of those lessons with stories about her ancestors. His firm commitment to ethical standards appears in *Song of the Trees, Roll of Thunder,* and *Let the Circle Be Unbroken.* In one scene in the latter book, Cassie had been warned more than once to stop playing marbles. When her father caught her at it again, she knew that she was in trouble because "what Papa promised, Papa gave" (*Circle,* 15). As Wilbert Taylor did, Papa Logan established and enforced rules in his family, including rules designed to protect his children. In *Roll of Thunder, Let the Circle Be Unbroken, The Road to Memphis,* and *The Friendship,* Cassie mentions several times that their father had forbidden them from going to the Wallace store. When Cassie is harassed by some white boys in *Road to Memphis,* Papa Logan is there to save her and at the same time gently rebuke her for walking the roads alone. "You s'posed to be at church, not walking the roads."[5] Wilbert Taylor the family man is embodied by David Logan, a man who protects and loves his children, as many family scenes in the Logan books show, including a scene in *Let the Circle Be Unbroken* where Papa invites Little Man to read with him: "I 'spect you best get your book and come sit over here closer to me and this fire and get yourself warm" (*Circle,* 41).

Taylor has told how soon after she was born, her father came home angry because of a racist incident at work. A similar event occurs in *Let the Circle Be Unbroken.* In this case, Papa Logan works in a sawmill for Joe Morgan, and one day Joe has been drinking at lunch and tries to start a fight with Papa. Papa is too smart to get caught up in a fight that would do him no good, "I didn't say nothing to him, just kept on working" (*Circle,* 315), stood up to Joe, and quit his job. When he came home, he found the "prettiest, baldest baby I'd ever seen in my life" (*Circle,* 316), the newborn Cassie. Just as Papa avoided a fight but quit his job when Cassie was a newborn, Wilbert Taylor left his trucking job in Mississippi to find better work elsewhere.

Taylor's character Uncle Hammer also has some real-life parallels; he is based on two of her great-uncles. Hammer's role in the Logan saga, however, is similar to the roles played by many of Taylor's uncles who lived with her family at various times in her life. These uncles were at times surrogate fathers, dispensing advice, love, and discipline when needed. Hammer was a frequent visitor to the Logan home in Mississippi, just as Taylor's uncles frequented her family home in Toledo, and while visiting, Hammer took an active part in the family, just as Taylor's own uncles did. For example, when Stacey lets T.J. trick him out of the beautiful coat Uncle Hammer had given him for Christmas, Hammer teaches Stacey a lesson about using common sense. Taylor recalls that this lesson is based on a true story. "This happened when my great-uncle gave a new coat to my father, and my father let his friend talk him into giving it up by calling him 'preacher.' " And as Taylor's uncles surely did, Hammer also contributes financial and personal help to the Logans in *Roll of Thunder, Let the Circle Be Unbroken,* and *The Road to Memphis.* Hammer also shares at least one other character trait with the Taylor men: "One thing Uncle Hammer couldn't abide was a dirty car" (*Circle,* 148). Tay-

Taylor's father with one of his new cars.

lor recalls many family outings where her father and uncles washed and polished their cars while the children played.

Taylor's books are also filled with warm and sensitive family scenes based on her own experiences: family meals, Christmas morning, a church revival, sitting around the fire in the evening, welcoming Uncle Hammer home or saying goodbye when he left for Chicago, including Cousin Bud in a family gathering, and immediately accepting his daughter into their home. What makes these family scenes effective in her books is not the fact that they are based on Taylor's own life, but that they convey the warmth and affection that she knew personally. As a writer, she achieved her goal to "show a Black family united in love and pride, of which the reader would like to be a part" that would make readers say, " 'Hey, I really like them! I feel what they feel' " ("Newbery," 405).

Her books are full of other autobiographical and family details. When Papa Logan tells the history of his family (*Circle,* 178–81), other than changes in names and places, it varies little from the history of Taylor's own family. One of Taylor's grandmothers was named Mrs. Lee Annie Bryant, and in *Let the Circle Be Unbroken,* Mrs. Lee Annie Lees plays an important minor role. The generosity of the Logans has roots in Taylor's own ancestors; for example, despite the great value the family placed on land, her grandmother was known to give away family land to family members and others in need. In *The Road to Memphis,* Cassie proofreads some newspaper copy for Solomon Bradley; Taylor herself worked as an editor/proofreader in Los Angeles in the days before her writing career took off. Cassie is bright and iconoclastic, just as the young Taylor herself was. Suzella Rankin, the mixed-race daughter of Cousin Bud Rankin in *Let the Circle Be Unbroken* is based on a cousin from Taylor's mother's family whose father was black and mother was white. Taylor met her one summer in Mississippi when the girl's father brought her South. Taylor's cousin looked white and was uncomfortable in Mississippi and wanted to return to the North immediately. Also in *Let the Circle Be Unbroken,* Stacey's running away to join the field workers is based on a true story of one of Taylor's cousins who ran away. Similar parallels to other major and minor characters and events can be found in all of her books.

A final parallel is the reaction of others to Taylor's stable, happy family. Many times in the early Logan novels, neighbors point out to the Logans that because they own land and have a strong, intact family, they're different from the rest of the people in their area. These comments nearly always carry a tinge of envy; the speakers admire what the Logans have and wish it for themselves. But it's not just the land these people envy, it is also the family. In *The Road to Memphis,* Jeremy Simms comments to Stacey about the special relationship Stacey and his siblings share with their father, a relationship that poor, abused Jeremy could only dream about. "All y'all's close" he said. "I done always been admirin' of that" (*Memphis,* 41). Readers of the Logan saga certainly feel the same way. The Logans, like the Taylors, are a close and loving family, one worthy of admiration and emulation, and most certainly a family that readers would admire.

The Pleasure and Pain
of Writing about Family

Though some might think it is easy for authors to write about their own family, Taylor finds it difficult and sometimes painful: "Writing is a very lonely business. It is also a very terrifying one emotionally if a writer knows and cares about the people of her novel as well as I know and care about the Logans" ("Newbery," 406). The Logans are, of course, essentially the Taylors, and for Taylor to tell the stories she tells, she must relive the pain her family has suffered along with the pleasure they have created. Though it is extremely difficult for her to write about her family, she continues to do so because of her desire to leave a legacy for her own family and for readers young and old who appreciate and perhaps yearn for the warmth of positive family relationships. When Taylor was young, she didn't realize that her family was different from most and assumed that all children had strong and loving parents and were surrounded by loving uncles, aunts, and other relatives who felt like parents. She also took for granted her large extended family and the many trips her family took annually to visit relatives. Though she now realizes how lucky she was, there was also a time when she took for granted the constant support her family provided as well as the family stories she had heard as a child.

Taylor claims that her family is not unique, but anyone who knows her or her family would immediately disagree. From her family she received a heritage that most people would envy: stability, love, and "legacies of the land and the stories of family and community history" (*SAAS*, 285). The lands her great-grandparents settled nearly 100 years ago are still owned by the family, and of course, the family history, preserved and shared by storytelling relatives, is also a part of her legacy, a legacy she has shared with readers by making parts of it the history of the Logan family.

In recent years, Taylor has struggled because of the pain she must endure when as a writer she must resurrect the world of her childhood in order to create her stories. Memories of the racism and violence of that world as well as memories of her father and other loved ones who have passed away are sometimes too painful for her to bear. At times, the old insecurities about her ability to retell her family stories and history with the power they deserve have returned, making her consider giving up writing completely. Fortunately for her readers, her family's example of strength and perseverance sustain her through these difficult times. She will continue to write, "partly because the stories and the history are part of my father's legacy, a legacy which has enriched me all my life. I continue to write because I feel the need to share that legacy. I continue to write because it is my hope that through my books that legacy will also help to enrich the lives of others. I continue to write, because by doing so, I can perhaps pass on a legacy of my own" (*SAAS*, 285–86).

3. Historical Context: Mississippi and the Civil Rights Movement

In her written speech accepting the ALAN Award for her contribution to the field of young adult literature, Mildred D. Taylor described, briefly, the essence of her books: "From *Song of the Trees* to *The Well* I have attempted to present a true picture of life in America as older members of my family remember it, and as I remember it in the days before the civil rights movement. In all of the books I have recounted not only the joy of growing up in a large and supportive family, but my own feelings of being faced with segregation and bigotry."[1]

One cannot read any of Taylor's books without facing, as Taylor has, the frustration, humiliation, and anger caused by racial discrimination. Though her books are not only about racism in the South, the racial inequalities that existed at the time her stories take place are integral to the conflict of each story. In *Song of the Trees,* David Logan must risk his life to defend his family's trees because a white man feels that the trees are, by virtue of his race, rightfully his. In *Roll of Thunder, Hear My Cry,* Cassie encounters for the first time racism and discrimination of various kinds. These encounters continue as Cassie and the world at large change in *Let the Circle Be Unbroken* and *The Road to Memphis. Mississippi Bridge* and *The Friendship,* though not directly about the Logans, examine some of the ironies of racial discrimination as it affects friends of the Logan family. The roots of some of the racial conflicts in these books are revealed in *The Well,* a prequel to the Logan books. Finally, in *The Gold Cadillac,* Taylor uses an experience from her own childhood to illustrate the various effects of racism on a young girl and her family. "In the writing of my books I have tried to present not only a history of my family," says Taylor, "but the effect of racism, not only to the victims of racism but to the racists themselves. I have recounted events that were painful to write and painful to be read, but I had hoped they brought more understanding" (*ALAN*, 3).

As a black child in the 1950s and 1960s, Mildred D. Taylor could not escape the profound influence of racism and the civil rights movement. Taylor entered high school in 1957, just as the civil rights movement was beginning to gain momentum, but it took years before any real progress was made. When men like her uncles who had fought against the racist Nazis returned from World War II, they found that the same country that had used them in military service expected after the war that the racist, Jim Crow policies at home would remain unchanged (*SAAS*, 274). In her family, she often heard stories of relatives who suffered in one way or another because of their race, and many of these family stories became the basis for plots and conflicts in Taylor's books.

As mentioned earlier, Taylor does not intend for her books to be only about racism and its related evils, but because her narratives are set in Mississippi in the days before the civil rights movement, each is unavoidably affected by the central conflict of the times for blacks in the South. Taylor's hope is that her books will help today's readers get a better understanding about a significant, but often forgotten, aspect of American history and culture: "Today, . . . younger generations have no experience of that time when signs over restroom doors, signs over water fountains, in restaurants and hotels said: WHITE ONLY, COLORED NOT ALLOWED. Today's generations of children, as well as many of their parents and teachers, have not had to endure such indignities or even worse aspects of racism that once pervaded America, and I am grateful for that" (*ALAN*, 3). So, in order to better understand and appreciate the roots of Taylor's books—and her own life—it is necessary to know something about the history of black Americans and of the civil rights movement.

A Brief History of Slavery in America

In America today about thirty million Americans can claim African heritage. The majority of these citizens are descendants of African victims of the slave trade that began to flourish when European countries developed naval fleets in the 1500s, but the exploitation of Africans as slaves has been documented to have begun as early as the mid-1400s in Portugal and Spain.

Given the influence of European culture on the United States, it is no surprise that the institution of slavery was established in the American colonies nearly as soon as the colonies themselves. As the colonies developed their agricultural economies, they, too, turned to the use of slave labor to provide the workforce for their farms and plantations; a Dutch warship brought twenty black slaves to Virginia in 1619.[2] The period from the mid-1700s to the early 1800s saw the largest growth in African slaves. One source states that by the late 1700s, blacks made up nearly one-fifth the total population of the United States, including almost 29 percent of Maryland's population, 33 percent of Georgia's, 40 percent of Virginia's, and more than 60 percent of South Carolina's.[3] As slave holdings in American increased, so did slave rebellion and escapes, prompting white slave owners to search for better methods of controlling and limiting the rights of their slaves.

Slavery was not limited to the Southern colonies; before the American Revolution, the use and treatment of slaves in the North bore little difference to practices in the South. Massachusetts was a notable exception; the relatively small pre-Revolution slave population there had legal rights and protection that were similar to those enjoyed by the white majority. In describing the conditions for slaves in the North and South, historian Thomas C. Holt writes that:

> [N]orthern slave codes were similar to those found in the South. There were slave rebellions in the North—indeed many of the first major slave revolts occurred there. Slaves were auctioned in New York City just as they were in Charleston, S.C. The punishments meted out to slaves for transgressions were alike, North and South: whipping, branding, and castration. Slavery

provided the basis for wealth and power in the North just as it
did in the South, and northern slaveholders also rationalized
their system on racist grounds. (Holt)

The early civil rights movement, if it can be called that, grew in
reaction to this mistreatment of slaves in both the North and
South before and immediately after the Revolution. The movement, limited mostly to isolated outbreaks of slave rebellions and
escapes, was actually less concerned with civil rights than it was
with basic freedom from bondage. The organized fight for civil
rights would not come until nearly a century after Lincoln's
Emancipation Proclamation freed slaves from bondage but not
from many limitations of their social and legal freedoms.

By the late 1700s, the nature of slavery in America gradually
began to change. The influence of the Declaration of Independence and other attitudes fostered by the Colonies' revolt from
England began to undermine slavery in the north. After the Declaration in 1776, a number of antislavery groups were formed,
including some in the South. At the same time some religious
groups began to campaign against slavery and call on slave owners to release their slaves. In response to the new attitudes about
human rights and slavery, many slave owners in the northern
states voluntarily freed their slaves. These changes in attitudes
towards slavery encouraged some blacks to use the new American
legal system to break the bonds of slavery. Steven Spielberg's film
Amistad documents one such case. In another, *Quok Walker* v.
Jennison in 1783, the Massachusetts state supreme court outlawed slavery based on the state's mention of equal rights in its
constitution. Gradually, slavery in other northern states also
began to decline. In 1787, the Northwest Ordinance outlawed
slavery from the area northwest of the Ohio River (Ohio, Illinois,
Indiana, Wisconsin, and Michigan) and the Southwest Ordinance
allowed slavery in the lands south of the Ohio River (Kentucky,
Tennessee, Mississippi, and Alabama). At the beginning of 1808,
the importation of slaves to America became illegal, and by 1820,
slavery was abolished in the northern states while at the same
time the practice grew stronger in the South (Holt).

Freedom—Without Civil Rights

Before the Civil War, the civil rights movement consisted primarily of isolated slave revolts, escapes, and antislavery campaigns. Holt points out that during colonial times and into the early 1800s, many of the organized slave revolts were encouraged by the hope of foreign support and refuge. For example, in 1739, recently imported African slaves in South Carolina rebelled and headed for Spanish-controlled Florida because the Spanish provided refuge for escaped slaves. In 1800, a slave blacksmith named Gabriel Prosser, hoping for support from the French and other antislavery groups, organized several thousand rebels for a march on Richmond, Virginia. Denmark Vesey, Nat Turner, and others at various times also organized slave rebellions (Holt). Unfortunately, most early slave uprisings had little effect on changing or eliminating the institution of slavery. In the northern states, the antislavery movement grew, including the Underground Railroad, which helped slaves escape to the North. In the 1850s about 20,000 slaves from southern states found their way to freedom in the North (Holt).

Slavery survived in the South because of economic need and because of compromises made between the North and the South in the framing of the American constitution. But in a country founded on principles of liberty and equality, antislavery sentiment grew over time. When Great Britain emancipated its slaves in 1833, the movement calling for abolition of slavery gained momentum. Abolitionists included whites and freed or fugitive slaves, including Frederick Douglass. Their efforts helped to make gradual headway against slavery and racial discrimination and to establish greater opportunities for American blacks. The first newspapers dedicated to abolishing slavery appeared in 1827. Benjamin Lundy, a white man, started *Genius of Universal Emancipation,* the first paper of its kind (Meltzer, 11). In Boston in 1827, blacks John B. Russwurm and Samuel E. Cornish started *Freedom's Journal,* the first black American newspaper. Other black-run newspapers, including Douglass' *North Star,* would follow. In the 1850s two black colleges were founded: Lincoln University in Pennsylvania and Wilberforce University in Ohio. These and other social advancements were encouraged and supported by black churches such as the African Methodist Episcopal Church (Holt).

By the 1850s, tension between the abolitionist movement and the government sparked numerous conflicts. Abolitionist groups worked actively to free capt red fugitive slaves and to undermine slavery whenever possible. Abolitionist John Brown organized a failed attempt to take over the Harpers Ferry military arsenal in 1859. Slavery and abolition were debated in private and public settings, in courts, government legislative hearings, and churches.

Though originally opposed only to the expansion of slavery, President Abraham Lincoln changed his attitudes toward slavery in general during the Civil War. In a meeting with a delegation for former slaves, Lincoln said, "Your race are suffering, in my judgement, the greatest wrong inflicted on any people. But even when you cease to be slaves, you are yet far removed from being placed on an equality with the white."[4] The northern Congress cleared the way for the enlistment of blacks in the Union Army in 1862, and in September 1862, Abraham Lincoln announced the Emancipation Proclamation. Soon, many former slaves joined the North's ranks and fought valiantly against the South. By the end of the Civil War, nearly 70,000 black soldiers had died in battle,[5] and 21 blacks received Congressional Medals of Honor for heroism (Holt). It was around this time in history that the fictional progenitor of the Logan family stories, Paul Edward Logan, would have been born a slave in Georgia in 1863.

When the Civil War ended in 1865, the Thirteenth Amendment to the Constitution was passed and ratified, legally ending slavery in the United States, freeing about four million blacks living in the South, and setting the stage for social change in both the North and the South (see Appendix A).

The period of change that was mandated in the South after the Civil War was called Reconstruction. The main challenge for the newly reunited country was to decide how best to "reconstruct" the southern states socially, economically, and politically. At the heart of the conflict was how the South would treat its emancipated slaves.

Many members of the governments of the southern states were reluctant to have the North impose change on them and resisted as much as they dared. For a few years after the Civil War, Union armies occupied the South to enforce reconstruction policies, but the presence of what many southerners still considered an enemy army angered many citizens in the South. To combat the influence of the North and efforts at reconstruction, some southern whites elected former Confederate soldiers to state and local political positions. Some of these leaders used their political positions to oppose fair treatment of emancipated slaves and to persecute blacks and northern whites living in the South. The federal government tried to help former slaves become self-sufficient by forming the Freedmen's Bureau in 1865 and by passing in 1866 the Fourteenth Amendment, which granted blacks citizenship and civil rights (see Appendix A).

The federal government's actions on behalf of black Americans prompted many staunch Confederates to become more militant. In 1865, a group of former Confederate soldiers in Tennessee organized the Ku Klux Klan, a notorious organization that terrorized blacks and white sympathizers. In another move to limit the freedom of blacks, southern governments began to pass new laws called "black codes" that placed various restrictions on former slaves with regards to legal protection, marriage, land ownership, employment, and other basic social freedoms.

The political battle between the southern states and the federal government over blacks' rights continued. In 1869, Congress passed the Fifteenth Amendment, which made it illegal to use race as a basis for denying citizens the right to vote (see Appendix A). Six years later, the Civil Rights Act of 1875 mandated that access to public facilities cannot be denied on the basis of race or color. Initially, these laws helped win some basic civil rights for former slaves, and during the early years of Reconstruction, blacks began to exert their newfound political influence. In nine southern states, hundreds of blacks held state and local political offices, 20 were elected to serve in Congress, and from Mississippi two,

Hiram Revels and Blanche Bruce, served in the U.S. Senate. During this same time, educational opportunities for blacks expanded greatly as groups such as the American Missionary Association established more than 40 colleges and normal schools, including Atlanta University, Fisk University, and Howard University (Holt).

Unfortunately, these gains in basic freedoms for former slaves in the South were undermined by the states' black codes and the economic oppression of sharecropping, tenant farming, and later by the "Jim Crow" laws that effectively overturned the 1875 Civil Rights Act and created harsh segregation in the deep South. Sharecropping essentially replaced slave labor on the farms in the rural south, where more than 80 percent of black Americans lived. Under the sharecropping system, white landowners would provide housing, land, and farming supplies to black families. In return, the families would provide all the farm labor and at the end of the harvest, split the crop, usually by halves, with the landlord. Sharecroppers, like many of the Logans' neighbors in *Roll of Thunder,* were cash-poor and had to rely on credit to pay for food, clothing, and other essential goods, while hoping for a profitable sale of their half of the crops in order to repay their debts. In most cases, sharecroppers could never earn enough to pay off their debts, partially because of low sale prices for farm goods and because of interest rates that sometimes averaged 60 percent. Caught in a downward spiral of low crop prices and exorbitant interest rates, sharecroppers found themselves deeper and deeper in debt and essentially in bondage to their landlords. Thomas Holt cites a statement from Ambus Gray, an Arkansas freedman, that sums up the sharecroppers' plight: "When the crop made 'bout all you got was a little money to take to give the man what run you and you have to stay on or starve or go to get somebody else let you share crop wid them" (Holt). Tenant farmers such as the Simms family and other Logan neighbors mentioned in *Let the Circle Be Unbroken* and *Mississippi Bridge* didn't have it much better. Usually tenant farmers owned their own farm animals and equipment and paid a prearranged portion of their crops to a plantation owner in lieu of rent for the farm land. The landowner typically kept the books, and it was rare for a tenant farmer to clear a profit (Meltzer, 222–24).

Although severe poverty caused many problems for blacks in the South, their ability to change their conditions was also limited by the increasing obstacles to voting. Shortly after the turn of the century, all the southern states had instituted policies or laws that made it nearly impossible for blacks to vote. For example, by 1902, the former Confederate states required payment of a poll tax in order to qualify to vote, thus blocking cash-poor sharecroppers from the voting booth. With a declining presence in the voting booth, blacks lost what little political clout they had gained early in the Reconstruction. Most southern states also required that potential voters pass a literacy test to qualify to vote, sometimes including in the test the requirement to interpret part of the state's constitution. This policy barred a huge number of poor and uneducated workers, again, mostly black sharecroppers, from the polls. A few former Confederate states implemented a grandfather clause, which allowed people to vote only if they had voted in 1867 or earlier or if they were descendants of people who had voted in 1867. This rule eliminated nearly all former slaves and descendants of slaves from the voting rolls because slavery was not abolished until 1865, and no slaves had had the right to vote. Holt writes that the overall impact of those laws was comprehensive and devastating to black voters: "In Louisiana, 130,000 blacks had voted in 1896, and they were the voting majority in twenty-six parishes. By 1900 the state's black vote had declined ninety-six percent; barely 5,000 blacks still voted. Only 3,500 blacks voted in Alabama in 1890 out of a black adult population of almost 300,000; 10,000 blacks voted in Georgia out of 370,000; 15,000 in Virginia out of 250,000; and less than 1,000 in Mississippi out of 300,000" (Holt).

A key incident in Taylor's *Let the Circle Be Unbroken* is based on the voter literacy laws; Mrs. Lee Annie Lees' attempts to register to vote is an accurate portrayal of the hurdles—and dangers— blacks faced if they tried to register. Taylor's story of Mrs. Lee Annie is based on various accounts she heard from her family over the years and is very similar to the actual account of Fannie

Lou Hamer, a Mississippi black woman who in 1962 was fired from the plantation where she and her husband worked as share-croppers for attempting to register to vote. Hamer was later shot at, beaten, and arrested for her involvement in voter registration programs (Meltzer, 259–63).

To outsiders, the most obvious signs of discrimination in the South came from the "Jim Crow" laws that segregated public facilities into "White Only" and "Colored." In 1896, a key Supreme Court decision, *Plessy* v. *Ferguson,* essentially overturned the Civil Rights Act of 1875 when it ruled that segregation was legal as long as it provided "separate but equal" facilities to both races. This ruling gave rise to a plethora of Jim Crow laws that segregated schools, movie theaters, barbershops, buses and trains, restrooms, even drinking fountains and phone booths. In nearly all cases of segregation in the South, the conditions were separate but *not* equal.

The scenes in *Roll of Thunder, Hear My Cry* that show school life at the Great Faith Elementary and Secondary School provide some insight into what segregation did to educational opportunities for blacks in the early 1900s. Schools were in poor repair, and supplies, such as the cast-off textbook that Little Man rejected, were either in terrible condition or simply nonexistent. Black schools often received less than 40 percent of the funding white schools received for school expenses and teacher salaries. Because many students worked in the fields, the school year was considerably shorter, and most black students never even attended high school; not long after World War I, the United States had fewer that 70 black public high schools (Holt).

As Mildred D. Taylor's books about the Logan family illustrate, black families in the South were able to survive—and even thrive—despite the harsh conditions in which they lived. But even when they managed to overcome economic hardship, segregation, discrimination, and social and legal restrictions, a very real physical risk remained. As David Logan said in *Song of the Trees,* "One thing you can't understand, Andersen . . . is that a black man's always gotta be ready to die" (*Trees* 49). David Logan knew that even in the 1930s, blacks in the South lived under the constant threat of physical violence and lynchings. In *Roll of Thunder*, the Berrys from Smellings Creek were burned by white men who accused them of being too friendly with a white woman; Stacey Logan's friend T.J narrowly escapes being lynched by an angry mob. Such scenes were too familiar in real life as well. From 1890 to 1920, more than 3,000 blacks died at the hands of lynch mobs (Wexler, 23).

The Fight for Civil Rights

Given the terrible conditions in which southern blacks lived, it's not surprising that the organized efforts to fight for equal rights gained momentum over the years. Two early leaders—each with different attitudes about how best to obtain equal rights— emerged at the turn of the century: Booker T. Washington, who advocated accommodation, and W.E.B. Du Bois, who advocated resistance. Washington founded and directed the Tuskegee (Alabama) Normal and Industrial Institute and was a widely recognized leader and spokesman for American blacks who advocated a more pacifist approach in the fight for equal rights. In a famous speech in 1895, he called for an end to the "agitation of questions to social equality" and encouraged blacks to work for economic opportunity instead of fighting for equal social rights (Holt). Many whites praised his attitude, but many blacks felt he had compromised the blacks' position on equality. W.E.B. Du Bois believed that political rights had to be obtained before economic rights were possible and felt that oppressed blacks needed to be more militant in their efforts to obtain equality. In 1909, Du Bois and Ida Wells-Barnett joined other black leaders to establish the National Association for the Advancement of Colored People (NAACP), an organization determined to eliminate segregation and racial discrimination. Though the attitudes of Washington and Du Bois differed, each played a major role in helping blacks move closer to equal treatment in American society.

The range of reactions to segregation and racism—accommodation or resistance—are reflected in David and Hammer Logan's responses to racist incidents in the Logan books. David recognizes the importance of economic security that comes from owning their own land and, rather than jeopardize his land and his family, often goes to great lengths to avoid inflaming local whites. Rather than respond to unfair treatment militantly, David chooses to deal with racist incidents in courageous, yet subtle ways. Hammer, on the other hand, would prefer direct confrontation with those who threaten or harm the Logan family.

During the Great Depression, rural blacks in the South suffered to a far greater degree than did most Americans. For many who were already strapped by the constraints of sharecropping or tenant farming, Franklin D. Roosevelt's New Deal programs only added to their misery. When cotton prices crashed from twenty cents a pound in 1927 to five cents a pound in 1931, the farm economy suffered a tremendous blow. The New Deal plan tried to limit production of crops as a way to increase demand and raise prices. In 1933, the Agricultural Adjustment Act (AAA) implemented this plan by requiring that much of the cotton crop be plowed under and the land left fallow for the next few years. The government was supposed to issue benefit checks to pay farmers for their losses, but in many cases, landowners kept the money for themselves (Holt). Much of chapter 4 in Taylor's *Let the Circle Be Unbroken* discusses and demonstrates the negative impact that Roosevelt's Works Progress Administration (WPA), Civilian Conservation Corps (CCC), and the AAA had on farmers like the Logans, on sharecroppers, and on tenant farmers. Some of the events in *Let the Circle Be Unbroken* also parallel the historical rise of the Southern Tenant Farmers Union, an integrated union that was founded in an effort to protect farmers from unfair labor practices and government policies (Holt).

Understandably, black Americans grew weary of being victims of racial discrimination, and their frustration erupted in violence on some occasions, such as riots in Harlem in 1935 and in Detroit in 1940. The NAACP was joined by the National Urban League and other groups in the continued fight for civil rights for blacks, and even though their efforts made progress, it was small progress. A major victory came in 1941, when A. Philip Randolph organized 50,000 blacks to march to the White House to protest discrimination against blacks in the defense industry. On the day before the march, President Franklin D. Roosevelt met with Randolph and agreed to take action in the matter if Randolph would cancel the march. Randolph agreed, and Roosevelt issued the first presidential order for civil rights since Reconstruction, Executive Order 8802, which allowed all Americans to work in the defense industry. Eventually, more than two million blacks held jobs in U.S. defense plants (Holt).

An unlikely breakthrough in segregation came in 1947 when Jackie Robinson became the first black to play in the Major Leagues. He earned Rookie of the Year honors that year and helped lead the Brooklyn Dodgers to the pennant. Though Robinson endured racial taunts and threats throughout his first year in the Major Leagues, his courage and resilience combined with his spellbinding baseball skill to open the doors for other black athletes to participate in major professional sports. His widely publicized breaking of the color barrier in baseball helped bring to the American public at large the unfairness of racial segregation and certainly helped to lay the foundation for later civil rights breakthroughs.

Harry S. Truman, who succeeded to the U.S. presidency when Franklin D. Roosevelt died in 1945 and was elected president in 1948, campaigned openly for civil rights. In February 1948, he said, "The federal government has a clear duty to see that constitutional guarantees of individual liberties and of equal protection under the laws are not denied or abridged anywhere in the Union" (Wexler, 11), and he called on Congress to enact modern civil rights legislation. In July, he issued an executive order that ended racial segregation in the armed forces. Truman also created the first Civil Rights Commission and issued an executive order that established a policy of nondiscrimination in federal jobs. His civil rights actions angered many Democratic southerners, but like Jackie Robinson, Truman did much to clear the way for further progress in civil rights.

Not long after Truman left office, several major civil rights events took place within a three-year period. In 1954, in the case of *Brown* v. *Board of Education of Topeka,* the Supreme Court outlawed school segregation and dealt the first major blow to Jim Crow laws. Desegregation came slowly; by 1960 less than one percent of black students in the South attended racially integrated schools, but the Supreme Court ruling put all states on notice that segregation violated the laws of the land (Holt). In 1955, Emmet Till, a 14-year-old black boy from Chicago, was brutally murdered in Mississippi for whistling at a white woman. His death received national attention in the black and white media, as did the trial of two white men accused of his murder. Though the men were acquitted, the fact that they were tried for their crime established a new precedent that whites could no longer lynch blacks and expect immunity from the justice system (Wexler, 55–60). Blacks throughout America were outraged at Till's death and the acquittal of his murderers, and the national attention his murder received served as a catalyst for a civil rights action that had been simmering for some time. Later that same year, Rosa Parks refused to abide by segregated seating rules on a city bus in Montgomery, Alabama; her arrest led to a black boycott of buses in Montgomery. In 1957, the same year that Mildred D. Taylor entered high school in Toledo, Ohio, nine black students, under protection of the National Guard, integrated Central High School in Little Rock, Arkansas.

By 1957, after his role in organizing the Montgomery bus boycott, Dr. Martin Luther King Jr. had established himself as a leader of the civil rights movement. A charismatic and powerful speaker, he preached active, nonviolent action against racism. In 1963 he helped to stage mass sit-ins and other large scale acts of civil disobedience to protest segregation and discrimination in the United States and at the end of that summer led a march on Washington of more than 200,000 protestors that forced the government to pass new laws to establish racial equality. In addition to his other efforts on behalf of anti-discrimination, he led a famous march from Selma to Montgomery that put pressure on the government to pass the Voting Rights Act. King remained active in the fight for civil rights to the very day he was assassinated in 1968 (Holt).

Unfortunately, the events described above didn't immediately end segregation and establish civil rights, but they set in motion other events that would, finally, eliminate many of the racial inequalities that had existed in America since its birth. Much has happened in the civil rights movement in the last 50 years, so much that it is easy to forget how life was for many Americans. For example, a black student in Selma, Alabama, in an interview 20 years after Martin Luther King Jr.'s march from Selma to Montgomery, said this about the world of her parents' youth: "Try as you can, you can't believe that white people once treated black people that way. It seems like something that happened long, long ago" (Holt). Unfortunately, many whites did treat black people badly, and the events in Mildred D. Taylor's books recount some of the suffering blacks endured because of racism and segregation. Her books also reflect the heritage and history of her own family. The legacy of the Taylor family in Mississippi and the larger history of blacks in America had an indelible effect on Mildred D. Taylor. "Much of my life," she says, "has been shaped by my being born black in America" (*SAAS*, 268). And it is one of her hopes that her books about the Logans

> will one day be instrumental in teaching children of all colors the tremendous influence that Cassie's generation—my father's generation—had in bringing about the great Civil Rights movement of the fifties and sixties. Without understanding that generation and what it and the generations before it endured, children of today and of the future cannot understand or cherish the precious rights of equality which they now possess, both in the North and in the South. If they can identify with the Logans, who are representative not only of my family but of the many Black families who faced adversity and survived, and understand the principles by which they lived, then perhaps they can better understand and respect themselves and others. ("Newbery," 407–8)

4. "Will the Circle Be Unbroken?": The Logan Family Saga

In her Newbery Award acceptance speech for *Roll of Thunder, Hear My Cry,* Mildred D. Taylor said that she had more Logan stories to tell; she has kept that promise made in 1977, continuing her pattern of weaving family history and stories she heard during her childhood with relatives, neighbors, and places she knew as a child. She has published six books since *Roll of Thunder,* and with one exception—*The Gold Cadillac,* a book based on her own childhood in Toledo—all have to some degree been about the Logan family. Though *The Gold Cadillac* uses some of Taylor's own family names and seems in many ways unconnected to the Logan stories, Taylor considers it a part of the saga for reasons explained later in this chapter. Two of her novellas, *Mississippi Bridge* and *The Friendship,* focus on racial incidents that involve friends of the family and are witnessed by the Logan children. These books probably should be considered merely tangential to the saga. The stories about the Logans have not appeared in chronological order. Sometimes Taylor has chosen to move forward or backward in time to tell another part of the saga. For a better sense of their internal chronology, here is a list of Taylor's Logan books in chronological order according to their content:

Title	Setting	Age of Main Characters
1. *The Land* (expected 2000)	1870–80s	Paul Edward Logan is a young man
2. *The Well* (1995)	1910	David (Papa) Logan is 10
3. *Mississippi Bridge* (1990)	1931	Stacey Logan is 10; Cassie is 7
4. *Song of the Trees* (1975)	1932	Stacey Logan is 11; Cassie is 8
5. *The Friendship* (1987)	1933	Stacey Logan is 12; Cassie is 9
6. *Roll of Thunder, Hear My Cry* (1976)	1933	Stacey Logan is 12; Cassie is 9
7. *Let the Circle Be Unbroken* (1981)	1934	Stacey Logan is 13; Cassie is 10
8. *The Road to Memphis* (1990)	1941	Stacey Logan is 20; Cassie is 17
9. *Logan* (scheduled for 2002)	mid-1940s	Cassie Logan is in her early 20s

Taylor originally had plans for one more book about the Logans, dealing with their lives from 1936 to 1938, but after working on the saga decided that the story wasn't working and that Cassie had learned all that she had to learn in *Roll of Thunder* and in *Let the Circle Be Unbroken* so she discarded the manuscript. Taylor's next novel, which is currently in manuscript form, will be *The Land*. She says that *Logan,* scheduled to be published in 2002, will be the final book in the Logan family saga.

"Will the Circle Be Unbroken?"

In a few of her novels, Taylor reinforces family values by using songs to create a strong and comfortable domestic atmosphere in important scenes. For example, she uses lyrics from a song she wrote herself, "Roll of Thunder, Hear My Cry," as a prologue to chapter eleven in the novel of the same name; at a family gathering with the Logans, Cousin Bud sings "Lord God A-Mighty, Stand by Me" in *Let the Circle Be Unbroken;* and later in the same novel, the Logans gather together to sing "Will the Circle Be Unbroken?" before they pray for the safety of Stacey and Moe.

Cassie says the song is about family, love, and loss, and it fits perfectly the mood of the family at the time. In many ways, "Will the Circle Be Unbroken?" also complements both Taylor's feelings about family and the mood of most of the books in her Logan family saga because, like the song, her books are also about family, love, and loss.

The hymn, first copyrighted in 1907, is one Taylor's family would occasionally sing after saying grace before meals. With its focus on family, it meshed well with their own attitudes about the importance of family, past and present. Besides providing the title for *Let the Circle Be Unbroken,* the hymn also encapsulates the essence of the Logan family saga. The first verse recalls beloved ancestors, something certainly familiar to the Logans—and to Taylor:

> There are loved ones in the glory
> Whose dear forms you often miss,
> When you close your earthly story
> Will you join them in their bliss?

The chorus suggests the family connections, the bond that links generations across time, and looks forward to the next life when family members will enjoy a more peaceful existence:

> Will the circle be unbroken
> By and by, by and by?
> In a better home awaiting
> In the sky, in the sky?

The second verse harks back to the stories ancestors related about their younger days and their faithful lives:

> In the joyous days of childhood,
> Oft they told of wondrous love,
> Pointed to the dying Savior,
> Now they dwell with Him above.

The third verse, again recollects the lessons learned from ancestors and the responsibility the current generation has to live up to its heritage:

> You remember songs of heaven
> Which you sang with childish voice,
> Do you love the hymns they taught you,
> Or are songs of earth your choice?

The final two verses of the hymn describe scenes right out of a Taylor novel:

> You can picture happy gath'rings
> Round the fireside long ago,
> And you think of tearful partings,
> When they left you here below.
>
> One by one their seats were emptied,
> One by one they went away,
> Now the family is parted,
> Will it be complete one day?[1]

Verse four parallels two events common in the Logan family saga: family gatherings around the fireplace and the regular and painful farewells to their father when he left to work away from home for months at a time and to Uncle Hammer when he would return to Chicago. The final verse laments the passing of loved ones and looks ahead optimistically to that one day when the family will be reunited.

Readers hope that the series of Taylor's books that make up the Logan family saga will be "complete one day," but even with the absence of the Logan family stories that Taylor has promised, the books she has published form a cohesive narrative, an unbroken "circle" of stories as interconnected and interdependent as the Logan family itself, stories that, taken as a whole, represent an impressive body of work. This chapter will examine each of the books in the Logan family saga and discuss how each builds on or builds from other books in the "family."

Song of the Trees (1975)

You remember songs of heaven
Which you sang with childish voice

The novella is based on a Taylor family story about a tree-cutting incident on family land in Mississippi during the Depression. Taylor had attempted to write this story several times before finally discovering the character of Cassie Logan and letting Cassie tell the story in her own voice. Cassie is eight years old at the time she narrates the story and makes clear her great love for her family's forest and her trees. While her father is away working for the railroad in Louisiana, Mr. Andersen, a white man, uses the Logans' poor financial situation, Mary Logan's ill health, and veiled threats as excuses to convince Big Ma Logan to allow him to cut as many trees as he thinks fit for $65. Mary and the children oppose the arrangement but out of respect to Big Ma, allow the deal to stand. When the children discover that Mr. Andersen plans to cut down all the trees, they alert their mother, and she sends Stacey on horseback to fetch David Logan home as soon as possible. When David returns, he and Stacey wire dynamite charges throughout the forest, and in a suicidal showdown with Andersen and his cutting crew, David threatens to blow up the entire forest and everyone in it if Andersen doesn't immediately halt the cutting of the trees. With the plunger in hand, David stands up to Andersen, who thinks David is just bluffing. Tightening his grip on the plunger, David Logan says, "I mean what I say. Ask anyone. I always mean what I say."[2] Andersen finally backs off, leaving the felled trees on the ground. Cassie laments the violation of her forest, and at the story's close hears her father call out softly, "Dear, dear old trees, will you ever sing again?" (*Trees,* 52).

Besides beginning the Logan family saga, *Song of the Trees* plays an important role in the Logan family history for several reasons. First, it introduces the Logans and their values: David Logan's self-respect and courage, Mary Logan's patient wisdom, and Cassie's love and innocence. It also introduces the general conflict of the Logan stories: the constant threat from whites to the Logans and their land. And finally, as the foundation to the rest of the Logan books, it is often alluded to in later books, giving the Logans a chance to demonstrate both their own storytelling tradition and their history of using their wits to protect their family and land.

Taylor's first book earned attention by winning the 1973 Council on Interracial Books for Children Award; it was recognized by *Horn Book* for "the tone of black pride that permeates every page" and for its "description of a child's feeling for nature which elevates the story."[3] *Booklist* described it as "a moving story that manifests two simple, strongly felt emotions: a love of nature and a sense of self-respect" written in a style that "smoothly backs up the element of dignity in the story's message and in its well-drawn black characters."[4]

Taylor's first book appeared at a time when teachers and librarians were desperately searching for authentic stories about African Americans. Before 1975, only a few African American novelists had broken into the young adult market, most notably Virginia Hamilton, Alice Childress, and Rosa Guy; Walter Dean Myers' first novel, *Fast Sam, Cool Clyde, and Stuff* appeared in the same year as *Song of the Trees. Song of the Trees* differed from most of the previously published novels about American blacks primarily in its historical, rural setting. With the exception of some of Hamilton's novels, nearly all the other black novels were contemporary, inner-city stories.

Roll of Thunder, Hear My Cry (1976)

In the joyous days of childhood,
Oft they told of wondrous love

Roll of the Thunder appeared in print just one year after *Song of the Trees* was published, the quickest appearance of any of the sequels of the Logan family saga. As always, the basis for this book came from family stories Taylor had been told. The idea for this particular novel came together for Taylor while she was visiting her parents in Toledo on her way back to Los Angeles after accepting the Council on Interracial Books Award for *Song of the Trees*. During breakfast with her father and her uncle James Taylor, she listened as the two men told a story she hadn't heard before. It was the story of a black boy who started hanging around two white boys and how the three of them had broken into a local store, and how the owner of the store had been killed. The black boy was accused of the murder, and his two white "friends" were a part of the lynch mob that came after him. That story became the basis for *Roll of Thunder, Hear My Cry.*

Taylor returned to Los Angeles and immediately began work on the book, work that consumed her thoughts as well as her nights and weekends. About a year later, when she was nearly finished with the manuscript, her mother needed an operation and her father's health seemed to be failing, so at her parents' request, Taylor returned home to Toledo to help care for them. One day while doing laundry in the basement the lyrics to a song formed in her head:

> Roll of thunder
>   hear my cry
> Over the water
>   bye and bye
> Ole man comin'
>   down the line
> Whip in hand to
>   beat me down
> But I *ain't*
>   gonna let him
> Turn me 'round

She rushed upstairs to sing the song into a tape recorder so she wouldn't forget it. Later she went to her father and sang the words to him, explaining how the words had come and what they meant to her and to the book she was writing. She also told him that she knew that the book she was writing would win the Newbery Award. He told her he would be proud of that. Her father died eight months later, just four months before *Roll of Thunder, Hear My Cry* was published and ten months before Taylor won the 1977 Newbery Award (*SAAS*, 267–68).

Roll of Thunder, Hear My Cry continues the story of the Logan family. Set in Mississippi in 1933 and narrated by nine-year-old Cassie, the novel recounts a year's worth of incidents that affect the Logans and their small community. The children must walk several miles along dirt farm roads to attend an underfunded,

Taylor (right) with her sister Wilma around 1952. This hairstyle was Taylor's favorite at the time and a style she gave to Cassie in the Logan books.

poorly equipped elementary school. Most mornings, they are run off the road by the school bus carrying white children to their own, better, school. Tensions are high among the black families who live around Great Faith, Mississippi, because marauding white "night men" had recently burned three men from the Berry family because one of them had allegedly been looking at a white woman. The burning is just one of many racial incidents in the book; in protest of the abuse by the local whites and to help the local blacks gain some economic independence, the Logans organize a boycott of the Wallace Store. Unfortunately, the boycott accomplishes little more than to make racial tensions worse. There are problems at the school as well; Mary Logan eventually loses her job there and the resulting loss of income puts the Logan land in jeopardy. Amid the family and community conflicts, Cassie has some problems of her own, including dealing with Lillian Jean Simms, a racist white girl about her age. The central conflict of the novel concerns T. J. Avery, a cocky, trouble-making, attention-starved friend of Stacey's who becomes tragically involved with two older white boys, Melvin and R. W. Simms. The personal and community conflicts in the novel reveal the Logans' strengths—love, courage, and unity—and ultimately bring the family closer together.

In Taylor's first fully developed novel about the Logans, the character seeds planted in *Song of the Trees* blossom in *Roll of Thunder, Hear My Cry;* David Logan's courage is still apparent, but so is his love, patience, and wisdom. Mary Logan has a much greater role in this novel, giving more than her share of wise lessons and doses of love to her children. Cassie and her brothers, though still children, emerge as more mature characters, each with unique traits and abilities that set them apart from one another while at the same time making them unmistakably "Logan."

Likewise, the seeds of tension planted in Taylor's first book burst into full flower in this novel. Taylor presents the economic problems facing the poor during the Depression in such detail that readers come away with a personal sense of how difficult life was for poor Mississippi farmers and sharecroppers in the 1930s. The hopeless economic circumstances are compounded by the oppressive racial climate of 1930s Mississippi, and Taylor pulls no punches in portraying the harsh reality of life for Southern blacks. With the exception of Mr. Jamison and Jeremy Simms, all the white people in the book seem to be working against the Logans and their friends and neighbors. These two interrelated conflicts—economic hardship and racial oppression—became essential threads that run through all of Taylor's books.

Kirkus Reviews found much to admire in Taylor's portrayal of the Logans: "though the strong, clear-headed Logan family is no doubt an idealization, their characters are drawn with a quiet affection and their actions tempered with a keen sense of human fallibility."[5] Taylor's depiction of a strong and noble family has been cited by many other reviewers and has been an oft-cited strength in all of her Logan stories. A review in *Horn Book* admired the plot and realism of the novel: "The book presents injustice and several ways of dealing with it.... The events and settings are presented with such verisimilitude and the characters are so carefully drawn that one might assume the book to be autobiographical, if the author were not so young."[6] Of course, as Taylor became better known, readers learned that, in many ways, *Roll of Thunder* is indeed autobiographical, at least as it pertains to Taylor's family.

The success of Taylor's best-known book put her in a class with Virginia Hamilton, who in 1975 with *M. C. Higgins the Great* became the first African American author to win the Newbery Medal. In the same year Taylor published *Roll of Thunder,* Hamilton published her fourth novel, *Arilla Sun Down,* and young adult novels by other black authors Rosa Guy, Lorenz Graham, and John Steptoe appeared. The Newbery Honor books in the year of Taylor's Newbery Award *Roll of Thunder* were *Abel's Island* by William Steig and *A String in the Harp* by Nancy Bond; Jim Haskins' *The Story of Stevie Wonder* won the Coretta Scott King Award.

Let the Circle Be Unbroken (1981)

You can picture happy gath'rings
Round the fireside long ago,
And you think of tearful partings . . .

In this, her third book about the Logans, Taylor buttressed family history with U.S. history. The Logan family as developed in *Song of the Trees* and *Roll of Thunder, Hear My Cry* is essentially unchanged, but the story is driven more by outside forces than it had been in the previous two books. Institutional racism, which Taylor herself experienced and read about as a child in the 1950s, plays a key role in the novel. But so do FDR's New Deal economic policies, especially as they impacted poor black families, including Taylor's father, in the South. Regina Hayes, one of Taylor's editors, said that Taylor included considerable amounts of historical research in *Let the Circle Be Unbroken,* and the historical detail is unmistakable. T. J. Avery's murder trial, which grew out of his problems in *Roll of Thunder,* seems to be patterned after the well-known trial of the murderers of Emmet Till, a fourteen-year-old black from Chicago who was killed in Mississippi in 1955. Taylor refers to the New Deal programs, WPA, CCC, and AAA, and the AAA's crop reduction program causes the most direct financial hardships on the Logans. In scenes reminiscent of Steinbeck's *Grapes of Wrath,* violent conflicts between union organizers and union busters of the 1930s play a role in this novel. A final bit of U.S. history woven into Taylor's novel is the "Jim Crow" segregation laws, including segregated bathrooms and the disenfranchisement practice of an unpassable "literacy" test for blacks who attempted to register to vote.

Let the Circle Be Unbroken is the longest of all of Taylor's books. The setting is now 1934; Cassie Logan is 10 years old and somewhat wiser about the ways of the world, at least the discriminatory world of Mississippi. Though several narrative threads are introduced at the beginning of *Let the Circle Be Unbroken,* the central plot issue of the first three chapters is T. J.'s trial. Despite Mr. Jamison's valiant attempts to have T. J. acquitted and the overwhelming evidence that T. J. is innocent, the all-white jury convicts him with only a few minutes' deliberation. While at the trial, Cassie encounters discriminatory practices heretofore unknown to her: segregation (bathrooms, drinking fountains, and courtrooms) and institutional racism (the trial). These encounters foreshadow other events: Lee Annie Lees' attempt to register to vote, the complications of interracial marriages manifested in Cousin Bud and his daughter Suzella, the racial overtones in the anti-union near-riot in Strawberry, and Stacey's indentured servitude in the cane fields.

After T. J.'s trial, Taylor develops four major subplots in her novel. The first involves the problems that arise from the AAA's cutback orders and Harlan Granger's blocking of government payments to the Logans and some of their sharecropping neighbors. As cotton prices continue to fall, the farmers become more desperate, and that makes them ripe for the appearance of Morris Wheeler, a representative from the new farmers' union. His attempts to organize a union among the poor farmers of Great Faith draws anger and violence from the wealthy white landowners, who will resort to almost anything to keep the union out of their area.

The next complication is the appearance of Mary Logan's cousin Bud Rankin who, when he confesses that he has married a white woman, draws the blunt contempt of Uncle Hammer. His mixed-race daughter, Suzella, lives with the Logans for a time, and her presence provides many opportunities for David and Mary Logan to have long talks with Cassie about a variety of racial issues. Uncle Bud's presence in the Logan home also precipitates Uncle Hammer's almost violent reaction against the tenuous friendship Stacey and Cassie have with Jeremy Simms, which leads to lectures from Uncle Hammer and from David Logan about why blacks cannot be friends with whites. These talks go beyond the initiatory talks Cassie's parents had with her in *Roll of Thunder, Hear My Cry;* Cassie has gotten older, and the issues have become more serious and more difficult.

The third subplot is the desire of old Mrs. Lee Annie Lees to register to vote. Cassie helps Mrs. Lee Annie study the Mississippi Constitution in preparation for the literacy test, and near the end of the novel, Mrs. Lee Annie's attempt to register is used by Harlan Granger as the catalyst to instigate a public revolt against the farmer's union. The final subplot occurs because Stacey, in an adolescent misreading of his father's example, runs away from home to work in the cane fields in order to raise money to help the family keep its land. The naive Stacey doesn't realize that the cane field jobs are little more than chain gangs; young men who have been lured to the fields with the promise of relatively high wages soon discover they have become captives of field masters.

In many ways, *Let the Circle Be Unbroken* might be called a novel of disillusionment. Stacey discovers, nearly at the cost of his life, that one cannot always believe what one hears and that even strong, brave, young black men can still be exploited by the ruthless majority. Stacey's absence causes a rift between normally rock-solid David and Mary Logan, and David Logan begins to question, maybe for the first time, if his time working the railroad in Louisiana has been worth it. Mrs. Lee Annie Lees, even with her long experience as a black woman in a discriminatory society, is painfully disappointed to discover that the constitution she studied and learned cold doesn't apply to her. Cassie and Stacey's friend, Dubé Cross, initially believes the farmer's union will succeed and be his ticket to a better life, only to have his hopes dashed when Morris Wheeler is first shouted down and then arrested in Strawberry. The Logan children who, because of their faith in Mr. Jamison and their hopes for T. J.'s safety, believe that T. J. will be exonerated, discover by witnessing his trial how unjust the white justice system was for blacks in Mississippi. The character who suffers the greatest disillusionment is Cassie. In *Roll of Thunder,* Cassie was introduced to some of the ugly realities of the racist world in which she lived, but in this novel, Cassie must face even uglier, more upsetting realities than ever before. Her family and her own inner strength sustain her, of course, but in this novel, Cassie takes some big steps away from the naive innocent she was in *Song of the Trees* or even in *Roll of Thunder.*

Let the Circle Be Unbroken represents an important move for Taylor. Her skillful use of historical detail expanded her narrative and made her less reliant on details from family history and stories. Her use of U.S. history may have been the result of her father's death because, for so many years, the stories he told became the source and inspiration for Taylor's books. It may be that after her father's death, Taylor felt the need to turn to other sources to complement the now finite trove of Taylor family stories she held in her own memory. Another reason for the increase in historical detail may be that Cassie Logan had, in the first two

Logan books, achieved enough growth through close, personal contacts, and as a more mature character needed to encounter the wider world in order to continue to learn the important, and sometimes painful, lessons of life.

As the third book in the Logan family saga, *Let the Circle Be Unbroken* set a clear pattern for Taylor to follow with subsequent books. It is one thing, for example, to write one book and to follow it with a sequel; it is another feat entirely to pull off an effective sequel to the sequel. Without smacking of a "series" book, this novel maintains its connection to the first two Logan books by relying on the same core characters (the Logans and their closest friends), by maintaining key narrative elements (racial tensions and threats to the Logans and their land), and by making several references to events and characters in the previous two books. The Logan family and land history begun in *Song of the Trees* is continued, and sometimes repeated in this novel. Other characters—two of whom, Jeremy Simms and Mr. Tom Bee, would later provide spin-offs of the Logan family saga—are introduced or sustained in this book, and that helps to provide continuity among the stories. The favorable reception *Let the Circle Be Unbroken* received from readers and reviewers helped encourage Taylor and her publishers to carry on with the Logan family saga.

Reviews of *Let the Circle Be Unbroken* were generally positive, with some critics pointing out weaknesses inherent in sequels, and most noticing the harsher reality of this novel when compared to Taylor's previous books. In *Horn Book,* one reviewer wrote, "once more, the fear, the cruelty, and the bewildering injustice of a hopelessly racist society are transcended by a family's strength, self-respect, and determination. . . . the effect of the storytelling is intensified by a lean, understated style and made more poignant by touches of lyrical sensitivity."[7] A review in the *New York Times Book Review* praised Taylor's effective blending of history with fiction: "Miss Taylor provides her readers with a literal sense of witnessing important American history. Through a narrative laden with dramatic tension and virtuoso characterization we come, humbly, to understand what it was like when a white boy of fourteen could call a black child's mother by her first name and rightly expect her to answer him as *Sir,* or when an elderly black woman, hoping 'to qualify' to vote, might spend hours memorizing the state constitution under the tutelage of a nine-year-old girl only to be met with public humiliation."[8] Other reviews echoed sentiments from critics of earlier Logan family books: Taylor's Logan family is courageous, noble, and admirable, Taylor's language often approaches poetry, Taylor creates and sustains tension well, elements of the South's racist history are inextricably woven into the plot. After reading *Let the Circle Be Unbroken,* most readers eagerly anticipated Taylor's next book in the Logan family saga.

With this, her third book, Taylor established herself as one of the leading writers for young adults, along with other black writers Virginia Hamilton, Walter Dean Myers, and Alice Childress, all of whom also had novels appear in 1981. Her Logan books, however, differed from most other novels about blacks by focusing on historical and family issues rather than on the grittier, social issues many of her contemporaries were writing about.

Taylor's Short Books: *The Gold Cadillac* (1987), *The Friendship* (1987), and *Mississippi Bridge* (1990)

In a better home awaiting
In the sky, in the sky?

On reading *The Gold Cadillac,* readers will assume that this book is the only one of Taylor's that is not about the Logan family, but the author states emphatically that it is a part of the Logan saga. Taylor says that the family in *The Gold Cadillac* is the same family described in the Logan stories, but this tale is set in the early 1950s after the family has moved North. She decided to change the names—to names from her own family—to avoid confusion.

As with her other books, this story comes from a family experience, in this case a trip to Mississippi, but unlike most of the other Logan stories, the plot is drawn from Taylor's own experi-

The white house is the one described in *The Gold Cadillac*. The children running in front of the house are Taylor, her sister, and her cousin.

ence instead of from family stories passed on by her father. Young 'lois narrates the story beginning with the day her father brings home a brand new Cadillac. Though she and her sister, Wilma, are thrilled, her mother is upset that their father has spent so much money on a new car when they were saving to buy a home in a nicer neighborhood. Despite encouragement from her husband and the neighbors, 'lois' mother refuses to ride in the car until the father announces he is going to take the car on a trip to Mississippi. His neighbors and relatives try to talk him out of it, warning that is "a mighty dangerous thing, for a black man to drive an expensive car into the rural South" and that he might get lynched.[9]

The family makes the trip anyway, and although the father doesn't get lynched, he does get harassed by police and is detained for more than three hours while his wife and daughters wait in the car fearful of what will happen to him. Fortunately, he is freed, and they spend the night in the car. By morning he decides to leave his car with a cousin in Memphis and continue the trip in a less conspicuous borrowed car. When the family returns home to Toledo, 'lois' father sells the Cadillac. For 'lois the entire trip becomes an education in the ugliness of racism.

The Gold Cadillac appeared during a lull in Taylor's writing production and was welcomed by her fans. Valerie Wilson Wesley in *New York Times Book Review* wrote that the "in simple language, [Taylor] manages to capture both the ugliness of segregation and the strength and dignity it took to fight it."[10]

In the same year as *The Gold Cadillac,* a second Logan novella appeared in print, *The Friendship. The Friendship* occupies a special spot in Taylor's memory because it was based on a story she had not heard before, and it was one her father shared with her alone a few years before he died:

> The last most vivid memory I have of my father telling the story [of Mr. Tom Bee] was shortly after my return from a two-year stay in Africa. I remember how special that time was. There was no large family gathering; there were no other storytellers present. In fact, it was just my father and me. Everyone else had gone to bed. It was late, after two o'clock in the morning. My father had to be up the next morning before six to go to work, and I had to be up early too, for I was leaving for my Peace Corps recruiting job in Chicago. Yet my father talked on, telling the stories of his childhood, and I, as always, eagerly listened, not yet ready for sleep, not yet ready to have the stories end. Sitting by the living room fireplace, I heard each story anew. (*Boston Globe,* 181)

In *The Friendship,* Cassie, who is nine at the time, and her brothers witness a conflict involving Mr. Tom Bee and a white man. Mr. Tom Bee is an old man in Great Faith. When he was younger, he saved the life of John Wallace, current owner of the Wallace Store, twice, first from drowning and later from sickness. In appreciation, John Wallace tells Mr. Tom Bee that he may always call him by his first name. This situation is highly unusual because at that time in the South, blacks weren't allowed to address any whites by their first names, and when John Wallace became older, Mr. Tom Bee reverted to the local custom, calling John "Mr. Wallace." Years later, Mr. Tom Bee decided that he had had enough and began addressing and referring to John Wallace as "John." On the morning that the Logan children are near the Wallace Store, Wallace's sons and Charlie Simms are infuriated by Mr. Tom Bee's disrespect and shame John Wallace into doing something about it. After warning Tom, John Wallace shoots him, explaining immediately afterward, "this here disrespectin' me gotta stop and I means to stop it now. You gotta keep in mind you ain't nothing but a nigger. You gonna learn to watch yo' mouth. You gonna learn to address me proper. You hear me, Tom?"[11] Even lying on the road, his leg blown open by the shotgun blast, Mr. Tom Bee ignores Wallace's orders and continues to address him as John. Horrified, the Logan children wait for the second shotgun blast to end Mr. Tom Bee's life, but the shot never comes.

This form of racism is much more brutal than what Cassie encountered in *Song of the Trees,* and in watching the events at the Wallace Store unfold, Cassie learns many lessons about black and white relations in the South. The book stirred some controversy when it first appeared; some teachers felt that it was too painful and graphic for young readers. Others felt that although the book portrays a very cruel racist event, it can lead to useful discussions about racism and respect. One critic described the book as a "spare, bitter vignette of race relations in Mississippi in 1933."[12]

Taylor's third short novel, *Mississippi Bridge,* was published in 1990, the same year as *The Road to Memphis.* As Taylor states in the book's dedication, this story is also based on a story told by her father. A departure from the other Logan books, *Mississippi Bridge* is narrated by ten-year-old Jeremy Simms, a white friend of the Logan children who appears in several other Logan stories. One rainy spring day, Jeremy is sitting on the porch of the Wallace Store with nothing to do. He sees two black women, Rudine Johnson and her mother, come to the store and receive rude, racist treatment from Mr. Wallace and other white men in the store. By contrast, a white woman, Miz Hattie McElroy, and her

Taylor's father, Wilbert Lee Taylor, standing on the bridge that is described in the Logan stories, the same bridge that is the focal point for *Mississippi Bridge*.

young granddaughter enter soon after and are treated courteously by the white men. Miz Hattie and her granddaughter are waiting for the bus to Jackson; later they're joined by Josias Williams, a young black man who also receives verbal abuse from the idle white men in the store. A few minutes later, Big Ma Logan, accompanied by the Logan children, appears on the scene; she also is waiting for the bus to Jackson.

All manage to find seats on the crowded bus, and, according to the Jim Crow laws, the blacks are forced to take seats in the rear. Just before the bus departs, a large white family shows up expecting to board the bus, and the bus driver forces the black passengers—including Josias and Big Ma Logan—to give up their seats to make room for the whites. With the white passengers aboard, the overcrowded bus takes off down the muddy road, but midway across the old wooden bridge that spans the rising Rosa Lee Creek, the bridge collapses, sending the bus into the raging creek water. Josias and Jeremy are immediately on the scene; Josias sends Jeremy for help and heroically turns to the creek to begin rescue work. Despite Josias' efforts, many drown, including Miz Hattie and her granddaughter.

In a few brief scenes, Taylor creates a microcosm of racist society that concretely reveals the personal pain blacks endured in the South of the 1930s. They are denied fair treatment in the store, they endure insensitive racist comments and direct verbal abuse, and are first forced to take seats in the back of the bus, then denied seating in favor of white passengers. In this story, however, racism takes an ironic turn and the discriminatory laws of the South end up saving the lives of the black characters. The effect is powerful. As with *The Friendship,* some teachers and critics have argued that the story is too powerful, that it might have an adverse effect on some readers. A review in *School Library Journal* described *Mississippi Bridge* as "an angry book," but also praised it: "Well written and thought provoking, this book will haunt readers and generate much discussion."[13]

Taylor's three short novels appeared during a time when many African American authors had turned away from stories about racism to stories of the harsher aspects of contemporary life for African Americans such as Walter Dean Myers' *Scorpions* (1988) and *Fallen Angels* (1988) or stories that moved more to the mainstream of young adult fiction such as Rita Garcia-Williams' *Blue Tights* (1988), Rosa Guy's *The Ups and Downs of Carl Davis III* (1989), and Virginia Hamilton's *Cousins* (1990). Taylor's novels from this period use the same characters and historical settings as her previous stories, but instead of concentrating on her usual themes of family and land, these books focus exclusively on racism and its effects on blacks. The books' brevity and singular narratives pack their few scenes of discrimination and racism with concentrated power. It is clear that in these three novellas Taylor intended to remind readers of the personal suffering many black individuals and families endured in the years before the civil rights movement.

The Road to Memphis (1990)

One by one their seats were emptied,
One by one they went away,
Now the family is parted,
Will it be complete one day?

As she did in *Let the Circle Be Unbroken,* Taylor once again relied on historical research to supplement and expand a story based on her own family's history. Because this novel is set in late 1941 in the days immediately before and including the attack on Pearl Harbor, it would have been very difficult to neglect the historical context of the story. And although the news of the attack on Pearl Harbor receives little play in the story, the world events of the time did affect the characters and their future plans. Taylor uses the character of lawyer Solomon Bradley to introduce Cassie and Taylor's readers to a bit of history regarding important equal rights legislation, including *Plessy* v. *Ferguson,* the "separate but equal" Supreme Court case that Southern states used as a basis for their Jim Crow laws and a later (1938) Supreme Court case that countered it, Lloyd Gaines's suit for admission to the law school of the University of Missouri.[14] But the most prominent historical details in the novel are those that affected Southern blacks at the time: racism and segregation. Taylor has not made much public mention of family stories from this era, but her father did live in Mississippi during the war, and two of her uncles served during World War II in the armed forces overseas. Their experiences and attitudes from serving in segregated forces very likely influenced Taylor as she worked on *The Road to Memphis.*

When Taylor considered joining the Peace Corps, her family discouraged her. Her uncles who had served in World War II told her that they didn't believe that Kennedy's famous call to service, "Ask not what your country can do for you, ask what you can do for your country," applied to blacks. Citing as an example their second-class treatment in segregated forces during the war, her uncles felt that for generations, blacks had done much for the country, but the United States did very little in return (*SAAS*, 279). Their bitterness may have combined with Taylor's own feelings growing out of the segregation and racism she witnessed as a child, the way she had been treated in white schools as a child, and her own weariness as an adult who had worked actively to promote equal rights for blacks only to see very little progress. Certainly, the tone of *The Road to Memphis* is unlike Taylor's other Logan family books. It's angrier, more frustrated, even bitter, and it is highly likely that this more realistic tone is a reflection of Taylor and her family's lifelong experiences of living and working in a discriminatory society.

The Road to Memphis is set in 1941; Cassie is now 17 years old and attending high school in Jackson, where Stacey, who is 20, also lives and works. Although this novel is her second longest book, the story spans the shortest time frame of Taylor's three full-length Logan novels. Both *Roll of Thunder, Hear My Cry* and *Let the Circle Be Unbroken* covered about a year, but *The Road to Memphis* covers less than three months. The story wastes no time establishing its focus: the ugliness of racism. In the first chapter, Cassie and her younger brothers are waiting near the Wallace Store for Stacey's bus to come in from Jackson. An overweight and good-natured friend of the Logan children, Harris Mitchum, goes to the Wallace Store to buy shells for a coon hunt, and while there, he is tormented and humiliated by three cousins of Jeremy Simms: Leon, Statler, and Troy Aames. Their treatment of Harris reveals their cruelty and inherent evil, and it also foreshadows worse treatment that Harris will receive from them and that Cassie, Stacey, and their friends will face from the Aames brothers and other racists through the course of the novel.

The main event of the novel, Cassie and Stacey's trip to Memphis, is prompted by a racial incident in Strawberry. The two oldest Logan children are with three of their friends, Little Willie, Moe, and Clarence, who have joined them to ride back to Jackson following Reverend Gabson's funeral. While stopped at a garage to repair a tire, Moe is verbally abused and humiliated by the three Aames brothers. Badgered beyond the point of self-control, Moe strikes out in anger, severely beating all three boys. Jeremy

Simms helps Moe escape by hiding him in the back of his family's pickup truck and driving him to Jackson to rendezvous with Stacey, Cassie, Little Willie, and Clarence. The five young people realize that Moe is not safe in Jackson nor anywhere in the South and decide that for Moe's protection they will drive through the night to Memphis, where they will put him on a train to Chicago.

Before they leave Jackson, Cassie has a brief encounter with the handsome, well-educated, and successful Solomon Bradley, a character who will prove to be their benefactor once they arrive in Memphis. Getting to Memphis, however, is no easy task. Stopped at a gas station along the way, Stacey is harassed by white men and Cassie is nearly beaten for attempting to use a "white only" bathroom. While trying to outrun their tormentors, Stacey takes his car onto dirt side roads where he does manage to elude their pursuers but damages his car in the process. Cassie spends a restless night trying to sleep in the car while her old fears of night men terrorize her. The situation is complicated by the fact that the headaches Clarence began to complain about before their trip have increased in frequency and intensity. In the morning, after Stacey repairs his car, they take Clarence to a local hospital, but he is refused treatment because he is black. The Logans find a benevolent black woman, also reputed to be a healer, with whom they leave Clarence as they continue their trip to Memphis. The Logans and Little Willie finally get to Memphis with Moe, and with the assistance of Solomon Bradley are able to put Moe on a train to Chicago where he will be met by Uncle Hammer.

When they return for Clarence, they discover he has died of a brain hemorrhage. Stacey, Cassie, and Little Willie return home laden with sadness over the loss of two of their good friends: Clarence is dead and Moe is in exile in the North. When they arrive in Strawberry, Stacey sees that the sheriff has Harris Mitchum in custody, and knowing that Harris has been blamed for helping Moe escape Strawberry, stops to see if they can help. Harris' sister, desperate to protect her brother, tells the sheriff that it was Jeremy Simms, not Harris, who helped Moe escape. Her announcement leads to one of the most painful scenes in all of Taylor's books. In the presence of the sheriff, his father, and his racist cousins, Jeremy confesses that he had helped Moe escape, and his confession triggers a vicious and frightful outburst from Jeremy's father. Charlie Simms pommels Jeremy, then, his voice laced with contempt and raw hatred, unleashes a verbal beating before he finally disowns his son: "Don't you never again let me see you in this life, boy. Can't stand the sight of ya" (*Memphis*, 275). The novel ends with a bittersweet reunion at the Logan home, interrupted by a brief visit from Jeremy who has come to bid farewell to Stacey and the Logans before he leaves Great Faith to enlist in the military. Jeremy is the final loss for Stacey and Cassie.

The Road to Memphis is Taylor's harshest novel, one where she lets the pain of loss and the suffering caused by racism hit the reader full force. In earlier Logan stories, the ugliness of racist incidents were tempered by the loving and protective cocoon spun by David and Mary Logan to protect their children and indirectly, to protect Taylor's readers. Now that Cassie and Stacey are older and more independent, they can no longer depend on their parents and family to shield them from the ugliness of life. Taylor's more direct presentation of the repulsive and hurtful effects of racism make this book unpleasant at times, but the novel leaves a lasting impression on readers that is equal to, though more painful than, Taylor's family themes that grew out of her earlier books in the Logan family saga.

The Aames brothers are clearly the bad guys in this novel; their malevolent "fun" at the expense of Harris and Moe causes suffering and other repercussions far beyond their puny imaginations. It is difficult for readers to avoid despising the Aames brothers, Charlie Simms, and the other abusive racists in the novel, and perhaps that is Taylor's intent. There are plenty of racists in her other books, but they rarely come across as so completely irredeemable and devoid of basic humanity as do the villains in *The Road to Memphis*. This may be partially explained in Taylor's ALAN Award acceptance speech when she said, "In the writing of my books I have tried to present not only a history of my family, but the effect of racism, not only to the victims of racism but to the racists themselves" (*ALAN*, 3). Of all her Logan books to date,

The Road to Memphis effectively, even painfully, shows the effects of racism on its victims, but in addition to that, it is Taylor's most powerful indictment of the dehumanizing effects racism can have on racists. The abuse the Aames brothers inflict on Harris, Moe, and others is ample evidence that they don't have a shred of humanity or conscience, and their lack of those essential qualities makes them less than human. Charlie Simms is even worse; his irrational bigotry and hatred of blacks cause him to lose all natural affection and dehumanize him to the point that he publicly beats and then disowns his gentle and good-hearted son. Despite the brutal scenes in this novel, Taylor adroitly manages her portrayal of the dual effects of racism to avoid overwhelming the reader. The tone of this novel is definitely more bitter than Taylor's previous books, but by using the fair-minded Cassie as her narrator, Taylor maintains a narrative objectivity that makes it impossible to accuse her of being vindictive, manipulative, or unfair in her presentation of racist incidents in the novel.

Critical reception of this novel has not been as universally favorable as that of many of Taylor's other books, but it still managed to win some awards and to receive praise for its effective continuation of the Logan family saga. Joel Chaston in *Beacham's Guide to Literature for Young Adults* joined others in noting how one key difference in this book, Cassie's age, makes the novel essentially different from Taylor's other books. "*The Road to Memphis* is itself an important book because it lets readers see characters from Taylor's earlier books as they are on the verge of becoming adults. Cassie and Stacey are no longer able to hide behind their father, David Logan, and go on a journey during which they must confront racial hatred directly.... this is a bleaker book than some of the earlier Logan stories."[15] For Taylor, however, it is a necessary bleakness because Cassie—and many of Taylor's readers—need to learn the painful lessons taught in a racist society.

In the same year, 1990, that *Road to Memphis* appeared, seven other young adult novels by black writers were published, including the debut novel of Jacqueline Woodson, *Last Summer with Maizon*. For *Road to Memphis* Taylor received the American

Library Association's Coretta Scott King author award, given annually to a black author "who promotes understanding and appreciation of culture and contributions of all people." The Coretta Scott King Honor awards that year went to Angela Johnson's *When I am Old Like You* and Jim Haskins' *Black Dance in America*.

The Well (1995)

> There are loved ones in the glory
> Whose dear forms you often miss

In Taylor's most recent book, the novella *The Well: David's Story*, she reverts to the format of her earlier books, basing events more centrally on a family story, leaving the book unfettered by additional historical detail. The narrator of the story is 10-year-old David Logan, the boy who later would become Cassie Logan's father. His story is one, as Taylor explains in her author's note, that her own family had shared with her. The setting of the story is the early home Taylor's great-grandfather had established in Mississippi near the turn of the century; the characters are based on Taylor's own family and people in family tales, and the conflict arises from the more personal racism of assumed superiority rather than the institutional racism found in *Let the Circle Be Unbroken* and *The Road to Memphis*. Because Taylor probably had little personal experience with this type of racial conflict, it is likely that she drew upon family memories to develop the tensions in the plot.

The Well is a prequel to the existing Logan family saga. Set in Mississippi in 1910, it is the story, narrated by young David Logan, of a hot, rainless summer when all the wells in the community have run dry, except for the Logans' well. Members of this earlier generation are as benevolent and noble as the next generation featured in the rest of the family saga, and they gladly share their well with all their neighbors—black and white. The story begins with David explaining the drought and his family's tradition of sharing what they have, even though sharing is sometimes hard to do, "especially when some of the folks you had to share with were folks the likes of Charlie Simms and his family, folks who hated your guts."[16] When the Simms come to take some water, they are met by the truculent Hammer. Feisty even at 13, Hammer refuses to kowtow to the Simms' rude treatment and challenges their right to Logan water. His mother intercedes, telling him that the Simms are welcome to the water and threatening Hammer with a strapping if he causes any more trouble.

But Hammer's pride and his fiery temper destine him for conflict. The next day, David and Hammer join a friend, John Henry, to drive some of their cattle to the Rosa Lee Creek to water them. When they arrive at the creek they discover that Charlie Simms with three other white boys and dim-witted Joe McCalister, a black friend of the Logans, have gotten there first. Charlie accuses the Logans of being "uppity," thinking they're as good as white folks just because they own cattle and land. Hammer provokes Charlie by reminding him that the Logans do indeed have their own cattle and land, things the Simms don't have—and their own water too, water that the white racist Simms have had to borrow from the black Logans. Hammer's retort is nearly too much for Charlie to take, and he threatens, "Well don't y'all go gettin' so prideful 'bout that water, nigger! Maybe one day you won't have it! Maybe one day y'all'll find somethin' dead floatin' in it!" (*Well*, 25). Charlie orders the Logans to leave, and to David's relief, they do.

A few days later while Hammer and David are on their way home, they meet Charlie Simms with his family's wagon, stuck in the ditch with one wheel off. Charlie belligerently orders the Logan boys to help him; Hammer refuses, but to avoid trouble, David agrees to help. Charlie makes David hold the wagon up to make room to remount the wheel, but Charlie takes too long to put the wheel back on and when David can no longer bear the weight of the wagon, her lets it drop, knocking Charlie back into the ditch. Angered and embarrassed, Charlie punches David in the jaw, inciting Hammer to fight. Hammer thrashes Charlie, leaving him unconscious, perhaps dead. David is terrified; he knows that a black boy could be lynched for hitting a white boy.

It turns out that Charlie was only knocked unconscious, but to cover his embarrassment at being beat up by a black, a younger black, Charlie tells his father that Hammer and David had jumped him, beating him with a piece of lumber. Mr. Simms reports the incident to the sheriff, who visits the Logans to investigate. Caroline Logan, the boys' mother, has known the sheriff for some time and by plying him with good reason and her good food, convinces the sheriff that her boys really haven't done anything. He believes Caroline but points out that the code of the South demands something be done, and offers to suggest to Mr. Simms that the Logan boys work on the Simms' farm for the summer if the Simms won't press charges. Just as the sheriff is leaving, the Simms show up at the Logans' home. The sheriff convinces them to accept his deal, and Mr. Simms agrees, with one addition. He wants the boys whipped. The sheriff can't talk him out of it, so the boys' mother ends up whipping them while the Simms family watches. Upset at the Simms, not his mother, for what has happened, Hammer vows revenge.

David and Hammer work on the Simms' farm every day, having to complete their own chores at home early in the morning and late at night. It's exhausting work, made worse by the constant taunting of Charlie and Ed-Rose Simms. When David and Hammer's father returns from his lumbering work in Natchez Trace, he explains to his sons that, as much as he would like to, he cannot do anything about the situation they're in. He tells them to learn from it, to remember that sometimes their lives are worth more than their pride, and to learn "how to use your heads, not your fists, when it comes to white folks. You learn to outsmart them, 'cause in the end you can't outfight them, not with your fists" (*Well,* 72–73). The boys work the rest of the summer on the Simms' farm without incident.

A week after David and Hammer have completed their "sentence," they return to the Simms' farm, and Hammer knocks Charlie down again, this time challenging him to tell Mr. Simms that Hammer did it alone, with his fists and nothing else. Hammer knows that even if Mr. Simms comes after him, Charlie himself will get a beating for letting a younger black boy beat him.

Charlie is furious about the beating and threatens to get even, but he never tells anyone about the beating he received from Hammer. Hammer seems unworried about the event, but David is sure Charlie will eventually do something.

Charlie's ill-conceived revenge is to poison the well by dumping chopped up remains of possums, raccoons, and skunks into it. His anger makes him blind to the wide-ranging repercussions of his vengeful act: spoiling the well hurts not only the Logans, it injures the entire community who depend on the Logan water, including the Simms. In a wonderfully just twist of irony, the novella ends when Charlie's deed is discovered by Mr. Simms, who inflicts public justice on him and Ed-Rose in front of the Logans.

With this most recent book, Taylor has managed to keep the circle of Logan stories unbroken. Even though *The Well* will not be the last of the Logan stories, it serves as an effective capstone to the Logan family saga by completing the circle of stories begun with *Song of the Trees*. In some respects, *The Well* is reminiscent of *Song of the Trees:* though it is about twice as long as Taylor's first book, it is still short enough to be considered a novella. Its characters have the same family warmth and values as a generation later, and the book shares the basic conflicts of *Song of the Trees*—surviving and avoiding trouble with whites. Other minor details parallel *Song of the Trees:* the story is set on Logan land in Mississippi, Papa works away from home, a grandmother lives in the home, something the Logans own—in this case water—is something local whites want. The two books have enough similarities to make them clearly related, but they are closer to being cousins than they are twins.

There are essential differences between these two novellas. As a narrative, *The Well* with its more fully developed characters and plot has more depth than *Song of the Trees,* a result of Taylor's refined writing skills developed in the 20 years since she wrote *Song of the Trees.* In *Song of the Trees,* Cassie dominated the story, and even though the rest of the Logans were developed enough to be appealing, they remained relatively flat characters. David and Hammer also dominate their own story, but other characters, including Mama and Charlie Simms, come more fully into their own. The plot of *The Well* is more complex, allowing room for David's grandmother, Rachel, to tell the story of how her name was stolen from her and for Papa to tell about his own white father. These stories help create a framework for the racist events in the story and the characters' various reactions to them without detracting from the central conflict, Hammer's contention with Charlie Simms. The enhanced plot maintains a tension not present in *Song of the Trees;* from the beginning of *The Well,* it is clear that trouble is brewing, that Hammer's temper is placing himself and his family at risk. In *The Well,* Taylor also presents a meaner, more personal aspect of racism than she did in her first Logan book. Mr. Andersen's racist personality in *Song of the Trees* seems merely to motivate him to profit at the expense of the Logans, but Charlie Simms' malevolence is born of an inherent hatred of blacks and is directed personally at the Logans. Charlie cares nothing at all about gain; he wants to destroy the Logans. The differences manifested in *The Well* make it a more painful yet more satisfying story than *Song of the Trees* and at the same time provide ample evidence that the literary potential Taylor demonstrated in *Song of the Trees* has been fully realized.

Critics welcomed the newest addition to the Logan saga, and *The Well* reminded many readers of the themes and quality of writing for which Taylor has come to be known. A starred review in *School Library Journal* sounded similar to reviews of previous Taylor books: "Readers will feel the Logans' fear and righteous anger at the injustice and humiliation they suffer because they are black. . . . Taylor has used her gift for storytelling and skillful characterization to craft a brief but compelling novel about prejudice and the saving power of human dignity."[17] A review in *Horn Book* praised *The Well* for its powerful effect on the reader. "This novella," wrote the reviewer, "delivers an emotional wallop in a concentrated span of time and action. Focused and honed, it moves rapidly from initial confrontation to denouement. . . .Like all of Taylor's work, this story reverberates in the heart long after the final paragraph is read."[18]

The Well was passed over by the Coretta Scott King Award committee who gave the Author Award to Virginia Hamilton for *Her*

Stories and Honor awards to *The Watsons Go to Birmingham—1963* by Christopher Paul Curtis and to *From the Notebooks of Melanin Sun* by Jacqueline Woodson. Curtis, a newcomer to young adult fiction, also received Newbery Honor Book recognition for his first novel, which with its historical setting and strong, two-parent family compares favorably to Taylor's Logan novels.

The Logan Family Saga

Will the circle be unbroken
By and by, by and by?

Taylor's Logan books have some obvious connections, especially setting, character, and theme, but it is her more subtle blending of elements from among the separate books that bind them together into a true family of stories. Her prequel, *The Well,* establishes the essential nature of the Logans as well as the character of David, Hammer, and Charlie Simms. The events of the story help to explain David Logan's later antipathy towards whites in general and the Simms in particular. The lessons David and Hammer learn and the wisdom taught by their father are repeated in slightly different ways in later books. For example, Papa tells Hammer and David to learn to use their heads instead of their fists. David Logan gives Cassie similar advice in *Roll of Thunder,* when he advises her on dealing with Lillian Jean Simms, and later, in *The Road to Memphis,* when he reminds her, "Don't get so smart, Daughter, you don't use your head" (105). The Logan heritage of land so strongly established in *Song of the Trees* appears in all of the Logan books; *Roll of Thunder* and *Let the Circle Be Unbroken* make direct references to the tree-cutting incident from *Song of the Trees.* Cassie or her father often talk about the importance of land, and the history of the Logan land surfaces repeatedly in the stories. The importance of names, especially in the way they are used between whites and blacks, is introduced in Rachel's story in *The Well* and reinforced in the later Logan books when Cassie often notes that Jeremy Simms was the only white person they could call by his first name. The conflict over names emerges as its own story in a Logan spin-off book about Mr. Tom Bee: *The Friendship*.

Sometimes in the Logan books Taylor uses parallel incidents that connect the books in a kind of heritage of experience. In *The Well*, for example, Charlie Simms has a vehicle stuck in a ditch and insists that the Logans help him. A generation later, Charlie Simms' truck is stuck in a ditch, and he demands that Stacey Logan use his new car to pull him out. In *Roll of Thunder*, the success of Cassie's sneaky but very satisfying revenge on Lillian Jean Simms depends on the fact that Lillian Jean's pride will not allow her to admit that a younger black girl beat her up. The same incident happened a generation earlier when Hammer got away with beating up Charlie Simms in *The Well*. The heritage of the Logans' relationship with the Simms runs through all the Logan books, but the only good Simms in any of the stories is Jeremy, who appears in *Roll of Thunder, Let the Circle Be Unbroken, The Road to Memphis, The Friendship,* and in his own story, *Mississippi Bridge*. Jeremy is an enigma to the Logans, and his desire for their friendship at times troubles Cassie, Stacey, and David, but his steady presence along with occasional appearances by Mr. Jamison remind the Logans and Taylor's readers that even in the South, not all whites are bad.

Taylor will publish two more novels about the Logan family, one on each historical end of the saga. *The Land,* scheduled to be published in 2000, will be the story of young Paul Edward Logan and will tell how, in the late 1880s, he comes to leave the plantation home of his father in Georgia and to purchase the Mississippi land that establishes the Logan family homestead. The story will tell of Paul Edward's life on the plantation and of his escape and eventual settlement in Mississippi. The final book in the Logan family saga will be *Logan.* Set in the mid-1940s, it will take the Logan family through World War II and tell of the move from Mississippi to set up a new family center in Ohio. The book is planned to be released in 2002 to mark the twenty-fifth anniversary of *Roll of Thunder, Hear My Cry.*

Taylor's Logan stories occupy an important position in African American young adult fiction. Prior to the publication of *Roll of Thunder* books with black protagonists were only a small part of the national market, and many of the books dealing with blacks or black issues were written by white authors. By the mid 1980s, publishers began paying more attention to black writers and their stories, but even then those stories did not present a balanced view of black life. For example, even though during this time black female writers outnumbered black male writers by nearly four to one, there were many more male-centered novels than female-centered novels. Another problem, at least until the early 1990s, was that images of family in many young adult novels by black authors tended to perpetuate the stereotype of dysfunctional families. There were too many "absent fathers; too many sick, dysfunctionally neurotic or addicted mothers, too many children parenting themselves."[19]

Taylor's stories provide a refreshing alternate view of black life. In "The Black Experience in Children's Fiction: Controversies Surrounding Award Winning Books," Joel Taxel writes "it is a lamentable fact that within the existing corpus of children's literature there are precious few stories of the sort told by Taylor."[20] With their female-centered stories of healthy families led by a strong father and a strong mother, the books of Mildred D. Taylor have always been an exception to the characteristics of most black young adult fiction since 1968. "I believe in the old rule that one should write about what one knows," says Taylor, "and that's why I don't write about the inner city; it's a world I know very little about."

All of Taylor's books suggest that her attitudes about the importance of family unity extend from her own life into her fictional Logan family and even into the family of her books. She has gathered her Taylor/Logan stories about family, love, and loss into a warm family circle that gives her readers a broad view of the Logans while at the same time welcoming them into the circle, even if just for the length of one book.

5. Taylor's Two Themes: Family and Land

From her father's stories and from her family's heritage Taylor learned the symbiotic relationship between family and land. From the time she was a child, this lesson was impressed upon her again and again, so it is not surprising that two themes dominate all her fiction: Family is important. Land is important.

Even as a child, Mildred D. Taylor felt keenly how history books and the media misrepresented black families, and while she was still an elementary school student, she determined that she would become a writer who would present a truer picture of black families, a picture based on her own experience. Nearly everyone who has ever read one of Taylor's books would agree that in the Logan family she has indeed created a noble and model black family. In a review of *The Road to Memphis,* Rosellen Brown recognizes Taylor's efforts: She "paints an appealingly detailed picture of the warm family relations and the embracing communal spirit to remind us that black life, day to day, however troubled, is not the disaster it looks like when it is simplified by sociology."[1]

Whether simplified by sociology or not, for many years a stereotype of the African American family has existed, a stereotype perpetuated by many, but not all, movies, TV programs, and books. This stereotypical family is troubled, fragmented, and base, dominated by a matriarch, in part because she is a strong woman but also because of the chronic absence of a father. The stereotype suggests that the lack of a father's presence leads to a broken, dysfunctional family, which in turn leads to a wide range of social problems for black individuals and for society in general. Though

Mildred Taylor's family in front of the family home in 1901. Her great-grandfather is seated in the center; her great-grandmother is seated at left.

it is difficult to track down the specific origins of this stereotype, part of it has its roots in the institution of slavery, which for reasons of economics and of control systematically fractured families. While it is true that slave traders and owners often split up families, slave families were more unified than many histories suggest. One historian states that most American slaves lived in intact, two-parent families. And when circumstances broke up families, "there is evidence of an extended network of kin and communal solidarity that filled the gap" (Holt). Through the years, the tradition of family unity among black families remained, even though the forces that undermined their families continued in slightly different form. After the abolition of slavery, economic oppression, not slavery, forced many fathers to leave their families in search of jobs and security, and for those trapped in the cycle of sharecropping or day labor, the economic uncertainty contributed to stresses within families.

In Mississippi in the late 1800s and early 1900s, the Taylor's paternal and maternal great-grandparents were an unusual example of family stability, in part because of their fierce loyalty to family and their determination to survive but also because they owned land. In the stories she heard at her father's side, Mildred D. Taylor learned of the importance of land ownership: it provided sustenance, security, stability, and safety. Throughout their family tales, Taylor's father and uncles wove two themes, values that would become embedded deep in Taylor's consciousness, values upon which she would base her own life: the importance of family and the importance of land. In her family's stories, these two were so tightly woven as to be inseparable. Family matters because it is the best way to survive and thrive; land matters because without it, families can't survive. These principles were proven true again and again in the Taylors' experience and in the stories repeated through the generations to the younger members of the family. Taylor's great-grandfather ran away from his family when he was 14. A few years later, in the 1870s, he bought land and built a house on it. Though the house burned down recently, an uncle rebuilt on the same site, and the land is still owned by the Taylor family (and, incidentally, the well on the family land, the same one featured in *The Well,* still provides clean, sweet water). When Wilbert Taylor moved his family from the Taylor homestead in Mississippi to Toledo, Ohio, one of his first goals was to buy a house, to own a place where his family could belong. Land was just as important to the family on Taylor's mother's side. Her maternal great-grandparents also bought land in Mississippi, land on which Taylor's grandmother and mother grew up. A part of that land, shown in the *Meet the Newbery Author* video of Taylor, is still owned by the Davis family.[2]

When the Newbery Award provided Mildred D. Taylor with the financial means to own land, she also bought a house for herself. Having grown fond of Colorado and the Rocky Mountains during her student days at the University of Colorado, Taylor returned there and purchased a home in town. Some time later, she had the opportunity to buy a log cabin with acreage in the mountains, even though it required selling the comfortable home she had in town. Her friends told her she was crazy to sell her home and to move out to foothills in the country, but she was unable to resist the pull of land; it was an integral part of her heritage. Says Taylor, "Who we are as a family is connected to the land." Though her Colorado friends couldn't understand her move out of town, her mother and other family members, upon seeing her new home and the surrounding land, immediately understood and appreciated her decision. Taylor has loved owning this land even though ownership was not always easy. Just as the Logans struggled to keep their land, so has Taylor. In the early years on this land, Taylor had to work very hard to retain possession of it and once almost lost it, managing to keep it only through the assistance of her mother and other family members. She still lives in that house and on that land in the country in the foothills of the Rocky Mountains.

Taylor's love for the land comes in large part from the tradition of land ownership on both sides of her family, but she also believes that it derives from her ethnic heritage. Her great-great-grandmother was the daughter of a black woman and a Native American man, and one of her great-grandmothers was Native American. From their African roots, Taylor and her family share the desire to have something of their own, a place for family. From their Native American ancestry, they have inherited a love, even a reverence, for land and nature. Taylor's early ancestors retained enough connection to the tribe that they even had to, at times, sign off on sales of tribal lands in the South. To this day, her family values its Native American and African heritage, and that heritage has only added to the Taylors' appreciation of the importance of land.

For the Taylors, the land was never separate from family. The original family farm in Mississippi, estimated to have been more than 1000 acres, became the starting point for generations of Taylors. When Wilbert Taylor bought his first home in Toledo, it was a duplex large enough for his immediate family but also with plenty of room to share with relatives who would later migrate from the South. Mildred D. Taylor's own home in Colorado is large and spacious, with more than enough room for family gatherings. In many ways, the land became a symbol for the Taylors, a symbol of family because it was on the land that the family began and from the land that the family derived the means to survive and prosper through the generations. The land is also a gathering place, now more than ever, where the extended Taylor clan can assemble to renew family ties and to share stories of the past, stories of the people and their land, stories that create love and respect for their ancestors and reinforce the love and connections among the living Taylors.

Just as land and family are inseparable in the Taylor family culture, they are equally inseparable in the fiction of Mildred D. Taylor. Her Logan family possesses the same values her Taylor family possesses: family matters, land matters. Taylor has said that in writing her books she wanted to present "a family united in love and self-respect, and parents, strong and sensitive, attempting to guide their children successfully, without harming their spirits" (*ALAN,* 3). No one can read about the Logans and not sense, and even admire, the love, strength, and self-respect fostered by Big Ma, Papa, and Mama Logan. Taylor has realized that in addition to love and self-respect, her family gave her the essentials of history, community, and the legacy of land (*SAAS,* 285).

Taylor's use of family in her books is not unusual in American writers, and the wonderful and inspirational Logan family accounts, to a large degree, for the broad appeal of her stories. But for as much as they love families, Americans also love land. Early settlers often referred to America in biblical terms as the "Promised Land," and for most of the first two centuries of America, its citizens were preoccupied with finding and settling land of their own. Romantic poets and writers celebrated the beauty and wonder of this new land, and explorers risked life and limb to see first for themselves and later to report to their fellow Americans about the vast and unexplored frontiers. In most parts of the United States, especially in the agrarian South, land became synonymous with security and wealth. Even today, part of the American dream includes home and land ownership. This American cultural tradition when combined with the land-owning tradition of her own family is surely the inspiration for the prominent role land plays in Taylor's stories. Anita Moss suggests that Mildred D. Taylor's books are similar to the works of other southern writers who "idealize the yeoman farmer and his family as they labor in cooperation and love upon the land."[3] For the "yeoman farmer" David Logan and his family, it is indeed the land and the keeping of it that create for them the opportunities to "labor in cooperation and love," especially in the first three books of the Logan saga, *Song of the Trees; Roll of Thunder, Hear My Cry;* and *Let the Circle Be Unbroken.*

Of course, Taylor's books are about much more than family and land; the historical settings of her books make the racist laws and discriminatory treatment of blacks in the South central to nearly all the events that unfold in her stories. Other themes are developed to greater or lesser degrees in her eight books: the importance of hard work and education, the importance of love and self-respect, the importance of independence and interdependence, the importance of resisting racial and social inequality, the importance—and difficulties—of friendship. These themes add depth and variety to Taylor's work, but even with the important part they play in her books, it would be misleading to suggest that any one of them is central to all of her fiction. Instead, critics, readers, and Taylor herself have agreed that for all that Taylor's books may be about, it is safe to say that they are first and foremost about importance of family and land.

Family and Land in *Song of the Trees*

Song of the Trees introduces the Logan family and its 400-acre farm near Great Faith, Mississippi, in the 1930s. Times are hard, and the Logans are scraping by better than many of their neighbors because they own their own land and because their father is able to work for the railroad in Louisiana. Though the family members understand the importance of their father's work to earn cash to pay the annual taxes on their land, they ache for his presence. This short book contains a few warm family scenes—the children waking up and coming into the kitchen where their mother and grandmother are busy making breakfast, the children picking berries and playing in the forest on their land—but their father is noticeably absent and almost constantly in their thoughts.

The important role their father plays in their family is made clear when Mr. Andersen tricks Big Ma into allowing him to harvest some trees from their forest and the children discover that he actually plans to fell all the trees. Stacey, only 11 at the time, spends three days on the family mare to fetch his father from Louisiana to rescue the forest. That such a small boy was willing to make such a long and hazardous journey alone—and that his mother was willing to send him—indicates the commitment Stacey has for his family and the great need the family has for their father. David Logan returns with his son and risks his life in a showdown with Mr. Andersen, threatening to blow up all the trees along with the loggers and himself. David Logan's willingness to risk retaliation from the white community for standing up to Andersen and his willingness to sacrifice his life for his land and his family demonstrates the great value David Logan places on the land and on his family.

The story of the cutting of the trees becomes an important touchstone in the Logan family history, one that the family alludes to several times in later books in the Logan family saga. In Taylor's own family, an event like the one described in *Song of the Trees* actually took place, and her father's recounting of the tale made a deep impression on young Mildred D. Taylor. In the author's note to the book, she writes that *Song of the Trees* is based on a story her father often told, a story she listened to with rapt attention. "His vivid description of the giant trees, the coming of the lumbermen, and the events that followed made me feel that I too was present. I hope my readers will be as moved by the story as I was." Taylor's own version of the story includes some vivid, almost loving, descriptions of the trees in the forest, and the conflict between Andersen and David Logan create an intense and memorable scene. More importantly, the success of Taylor's version of her father's story established family and land as key elements for her later work.

Family and Land in
Roll of Thunder, Hear My Cry

In Taylor's second book, *Roll of Thunder, Hear My Cry,* the importance of land and family is fully realized. The story of *Roll of Thunder* begins a year after the tree-cutting incident reported in *Song of the Trees.* Cassie Logan, the narrator, is now nine years old, and as the novel opens she and her brothers are preparing for the beginning of a new school year. The four children are together, as they nearly always are, walking the dusty red road to the Great Faith school. This opening scene embodies the two Taylor emphases, family and land, by combining the togetherness of family as the children walk to school together with Cassie's poetic description of the land around them, the "narrow, sun-splotched road wound like a lazy red serpent dividing the high forest bank of quiet old trees on the left from the cotton field, forested by giant green and purple stalks, on the right" (*Thunder,* 6). At that point, to emphasize more directly the importance of the land to the Logans, Taylor has Cassie tell readers the story of the land. Originally, it had belonged to the Granger family, who sold it during Reconstruction. In 1887, Paul Edward Logan, Cassie's grandfather, purchased 200 acres from a Yankee carpetbagger, and when that land was paid off in 1918, he bought an additional 200 acres from Wade Jamison, a local lawyer and one of the Logans' few white friends.

Immediately after recounting the history of the Logan land, Cassie explains that because of property taxes and the mortgage on the second 200 acres, her father must work the railroad, and here, using a scene between Cassie and her father, Taylor once again combines family and land. As a child, Cassie knew her father loved her and her family and that they needed him at home, so she couldn't understand why he chose to work in

Louisiana. David Logan's attempt to explain to Cassie why he has
to work away from home reveals his love for Cassie and his strong
sense of commitment to his family and to the land:

> "Look out there, Cassie girl. All that belongs to you. You ain't
> never had to live on nobody's place but your own and long as I
> live and the family survives, you'll never have to. That's impor-
> tant. . . ."

> I looked at Papa strangely when he said that, for I knew that
> all the land did not belong to me. Some of it belonged to Stacey,
> Christopher-John, and Little Man, not to mention the part that
> belonged to Big Ma, Mama, and Uncle Hammer. . . . But Papa
> never divided the land in his mind; it was simply Logan land.
> For it, he would work the long, hot summer pounding steel;
> Mama would teach and run the farm; Big Ma, in her sixties,
> would work like a woman of twenty in the fields and keep the
> house; the boys and I would wear threadbare clothing washed to
> dishwater color; but always, the taxes and the mortgage would
> be paid. (*Thunder*, 7–8)

Just as David Logan doesn't divide the land in his mind, he also
does not separate his family from the land. For him, the Logans
and the land are symbiotic, each depending on and prospering
because of the other. And although the Logans must scrimp and
sacrifice to keep their land, it is their ownership of the land that
allows them the luxury denied their neighbors: to remain independent and together. By the end of novel, Cassie understands
her father's lesson.

With the foundation of family and land firmly established in the
novel's first eight pages, Taylor introduces a series of characters
and conflicts that over the course of *Roll of Thunder* impact
either the family, the land, or both. This technique creates a constant tension in the story, for the things the Logans prize the very
most—family and land—dangle in the balance throughout the
novel. For example, T. J. Avery, a troublemaking friend of
Stacey's, creates conflict for the Logans and their land in various
ways: he cheats in class but allows Stacey to take the blame; he
dupes Stacey out of a beautiful winter coat; he gets Mary Logan,

the children's mother and Stacey and T. J.'s teacher, fired from school so that her loss of income seriously threatens the Logans' ability to keep their land; and in a final self-destructive act, his association with two no-account white boys and the trouble they get into forces David Logan to set his crops on fire in order to save T. J. from a lynch mob.

Though T. J. is at the center of most of the storms in the novel, Taylor introduces other characters who contribute to the tension of the story because they threaten the Logans' most prized possessions. The speeding white school bus always makes the roads dangerous for the Logan children. Harland Granger, the wily plantation owner who lives next to the Logans, perpetually schemes to steal the Logan land. The Wallace Store is an economic and social threat to all the residents around Great Faith, including the Logans. The marauding night men are a constant physical threat to the family. Lillian Jean Simms and her father introduce Cassie to the cruelty of bigotry, and Cassie's reaction to them puts her and her family at risk. On a return trip from Vicksburg during the night, Papa Logan is attacked and injured by the Wallaces. When Stacey helps T. J. escape from the Simms and the mob, he and Cassie worry what the consequences might be. The Logans deal with all these troublemakers nobly and wisely, managing to overcome one peril after another. A key factor in their survival is their commitment to one another and to their home, which is summed up in David Logan's promise to Cassie when she worries that the loss of her mother's job will make it impossible for them to pay the mortgage and the taxes. Her father says simply and resolutely, "We ain't never gonna lose this land" (*Thunder*, 152), and he's right. Despite constant threats and tension, by the novel's end, the Logans and their land remain intact.

A final word about T. J. Avery: T. J. serves as the central tragic figure in the story. His foolishness causes problems for many characters but ultimately injures him the most. In many ways, T. J. serves as a foil for the Logans: what he needs and lacks, a strong family and the relative security land ownership provides, the Logans have. Through the character of T. J., Taylor accomplishes many things, including revealing the pernicious power racists wielded in the South in the 1930s, but perhaps T. J. serves to emphasize once again what Taylor—and her Logans—know so well: family and land matter. One cannot help but wonder how different T. J.'s life would have been had he been blessed with strong parents like David and Mary Logan. And it is entirely possible that had T. J. had the self-respect the Logans had and the sense of economic security their land provided, he would never have gotten involved with the Simms brothers. T. J. is indeed a tragic figure, but maybe what Taylor wants to convey to readers is that the tragedy is not so much a result of T. J.'s foolish flaws but of his unfortunate lack of a strong, landowning family.

In a single scene in *Roll of Thunder* Taylor beautifully and symbolically combines the Logans and their land. When the Logan-led boycott of the Wallace Store has fallen apart and it appears that the Logans themselves will suffer for it, Cassie asks her father if they're going to give up as the others have. David Logan pulls Cassie close to him and then points down the drive, telling her to notice a lone fig tree, surrounded by large oak and walnut trees that overshadow it. He explains that the fig has as much right to its place in the yard as the other trees do, and it survives because it has deep roots. The tree "just keeps on growing and doing what it gotta do. It don't give up. It give up, it'll die. There's a lesson to be learned from that little tree, Cassie girl, 'cause we're like it. We keep doing what we gotta, and we don't give up. We can't" (*Thunder,* 206). Taylor imbues this scene with the warmth, wisdom, and love of David Logan and through his words reminds Cassie and the reader once again of the importance family and land play in the lives of her characters.

Family and Land in
Let the Circle Be Unbroken

In Taylor's third book, *Let the Circle Be Unbroken,* the themes of family and land continue, though the book's many subplots make them less prominent than they are in her previous books. T. J. Avery plays a minor role in this novel; the first three chapters deal with some of the aftermath of his rescue and arrest in *Roll of Thunder, Hear My Cry* and focus most specifically on his trial. What has happened to T. J. clearly has affected the Logans, especially Stacey, and T. J.'s trial serves as a lesson to the Logan children about the vulnerability of blacks in an oppressive society and as a reminder that what they have—a wise, strong family that lives on its own land—may be their best protection against the evils of racism.

When T. J.'s story finally comes to an end, Taylor turns her attention to a series of subplots, all of which spring from family relations or from the Logans' efforts to keep their land. Mrs. Lee Annie Lees decides to register to vote for her sixty-fifth birthday, and the Logan family is drawn into the event because Cassie helps Mrs. Lee Annie study the Mississippi constitution in preparation for the literacy test she must pass in order to register. Another subplot begins with the appearance of cousin Bud and fair-skinned daughter, Suzella. Their presence creates several conflicts, most of which strain family ties and make Cassie ponder the wide-ranging complications of race relations, including interracial marriage.

Taylor relied on considerable historical research to generate the next subplot. *Let the Circle Be Unbroken* is set in 1934, a time when Roosevelt's New Deal programs, especially the Agricultural Adjustment Administration, seriously harmed most poor farmers and sharecroppers. Because of machinations by Harlan Granger and the AAA regulations, the Logans are forced to plant a smaller crop, which ultimately means that once again their land is threatened because they'll have less farm income to use for tax and mortgage payments. Farmers all over the South faced similar or more desperate situations, and in response to the oppressive plantation owners and the New Deal agricultural policies, an interracial farm union, the Southern Tenant Farmers Union, was founded by H. L. Mitchell (Holt). In the novel, a farm union organizer begins to lobby the Logans and other local farmers to join the newly formed union; unfortunately, his efforts only incite anger, retribution, and violence, which threaten the Logans and their land.

The worries the Logans have about hanging onto their land are the catalyst for yet another subplot, one that accentuates Taylor's family and land priorities. Lured by the promise of good wages and hoping to use his wages to pay the taxes and mortgage, Stacey runs away from home to work in the cane fields. His departure is catastrophic for the Logans. Because of his absence, the work on the family farm increases for the family left behind, and David Logan nearly loses his railroad job because of the time he spends searching for Stacey. The family has long had to endure the absence of their father; having the oldest child gone as well is almost too much for the close-knit family to bear. To complicate matters, Mary Logan blames her husband for Stacey's leaving, and her accusations, combined with David Logan's feelings of guilt and worry, put strains on their marriage that neither they nor their children have ever felt before.

These various conflicts provide Taylor with a number of opportunities to present scenes that reinforce her most familiar and favorite themes. As in most of her other books, *Let the Circle Be Unbroken* contains some picturesque descriptions of the land that Taylor and her Logans love. One particularly memorable passage describes winter around the Logan home in the Mississippi farmland. Cassie describes the winter days as "gray and still," days when people and their farm animals stayed inside and "nothing seemed to stir but the smoke curling upward from clay chimneys and an occasional red-winged blackbird" (*Circle,* 87). And although the weather was not nearly as cold as the bitter Chicago winters Uncle Hammer often described, it was cold, "a frosty, idle cold that seeped across a hot land ever looking toward the days of green and ripening fields, a cold that lay uneasy during its short stay as it crept through the cracks of poorly constructed wooden houses and forced the people huddled inside around ever-burning fires to wish it gone" (*Circle,* 87). Other scenes describing the fields, the forest, or the little Rosa Lee river epitomize the reverence Taylor and her characters have for the land.

The Logans' struggle to keep their land continues in this novel. Cassie's narration makes clear how deeply the family misses the father while he's working the rails in Louisiana, as does Mary

Logan's chiding him for his absences, especially because the adolescent Stacey desperately needs his father's presence. David Logan dearly loves his family and his home and would prefer to be with them if he could, but he knows that without their land, his family will suffer far more, so he continues to work for cash wages to keep the land. When his wife reminds him of how much his family needs him at home, David Logan responds that he understands that as well as she does, but that they need other things as well. "They need this land. Long as we've got this land, we've got something, something most folks ain't, and we can't risk losing it" (*Circle,* 187). Stacey has learned from his father's example, and it is Stacey's desire to help keep the land that drives him to the cane fields.

Stacey is not the only Logan child who has learned the lessons of the land. Cassie possesses an inherent love for the land that first manifests itself in *Song of the Trees* where she talks lovingly to the trees and describes the Logan forest in near religious terms. In *Roll of Thunder,* she is told the history of the Logan land more than once, but in *Let the Circle Be Unbroken,* she demonstrates that that story has now become her own. Her friend Dubé Cross asks her how the Logans came to own their land, and Cassie recites for him the story of how her grandfather bought the land in two parcels, one from a Yankee carpetbagger and the other from Mr. Jamison. Dubé, his own longing for that kind of security obvious, stutters, "Y-y-y'all some kkkk-kinda lucky" (*Circle,* 128–29). Cassie agrees and reflects on her family's good fortune. She looks around her house, a palace compared to the one-room, tar-papered shacks her neighbors live in, and sees not luxury, but family. The walls hold photographs of relatives. The furniture was made or owned by her grandfather. The rooms themselves are filled with loving memories of family meals, celebrations, study, and stories. As she did with the fig tree in *Roll of Thunder,* Taylor uses an image from the land, in this case the Logans' home, to symbolize the bond between the family and the land.

Several scenes in *Let the Circle Be Unbroken* reveal the great love the Logans share. Throughout the novel, there are several joyful reunions where the Logans welcome back with unbounded affection and enthusiasm various family members. Each time David Logan returns from Louisiana, the children smother him with hugs and attention. Each of Uncle Hammer's visits from Chicago is cause for celebration. Cousin Bud, initially a stranger to all but Mary Logan, is welcomed with open arms and automatically included in a family gathering. Suzella takes immediately to the loving acceptance she feels among the Logans and relishes the family atmosphere she has longed for but never experienced. These reunions and gatherings are cozy family scenes filled with laughter, stories, food, songs, and love. Perhaps one of the most poignant family gatherings occurs when the Logans gather on Christmas morning—without Stacey, who has still not been found. The void overshadows what would normally be a joyous event, and in a show of their love for Stacey and their concern for his welfare, the first thing the Logans do is to gather around the fireplace and sing "Will the Circle Be Unbroken," a hymn about family, love, and loss. Immediately after the song, the family kneels and each member offers a prayer pleading for Stacey's return.

The final and most touching reunion comes as an answer to those prayers. David admits that the family has suffered without Stacey, "We all part of one body in this family, and with Stacey gone, we just ain't whole" (*Circle*, 293), but reminds his family that even without Stacey they all have to remain strong and unified in order to survive the pain and suffering they share. The Logans have exhausted every possibility of finding Stacey, even enlisting their white friend, the lawyer Mr. Jamison, and now all they have left is their faith. Finally, thanks to Mr. Jamison's intervention and some lucky breaks, Stacey is found and reunited with the Logans in a round of "hugging and crying and kissing" (*Circle*, 383) like Cassie had never before witnessed. The novel concludes with Stacey arriving home again, this time being welcomed by Big Ma, his younger brothers, and Mr. Morrison. Here, Taylor uses the high profile final line of her novel to emphasize once again the connection between family and land and their importance to her and her characters. Stacey's

response to his homecoming is one of the last lines of the novel
and sums up the importance of home and family for Stacey and
the Logans: "I done come home . . . and it's the very best place to
be" (*Circle,* 394).

Family and Land in *The Road to Memphis*

In *The Road to Memphis,* the themes of family and land fade to
the background as Taylor aims her narrative more directly at
issues of racism and social inequality for blacks, issues that are, of
course, integral to her other books. However, this novel is the
first one whose central focus is not family and land. This novel is
set in 1941, seven years after *Let the Circle Be Unbroken.* Cassie is
17, and now more mature, an adolescent growing more distant
from her family and the land in many ways, including attending
high school in faraway Jackson. Other aspects of life demand her
attention; still, family and home remain important to Cassie and
to Stacey, who also now lives in Jackson. They return home as
often as possible, and it is always very difficult for them to leave
again for Jackson. Apparently, the Logans' economic situation
has improved significantly; David Logan no longer works on the
railroad in Louisiana, and no mention is made about their land
being at risk. In fact, other than several lines that remind readers
how much Cassie prefers the country, "where things were open
and clean and there weren't people the next house over practi-
cally sitting on your doorstep" (*Memphis,* 80), land is rarely mentioned.

One scene, however, is reminiscent of the previous Logan
books. Cassie has returned home for a weekend and is visiting
with her friend Moe Turner. For many years Moe, the son of a
poor sharecropper, has dreamed of escaping the stranglehold of
the sharecrop system and getting his own land for himself and his
family. He tells Cassie what she already knows, what she learned
at her father's feet from the time she was a small child: "It's
important for a man to have land, something of his own, and I
want my daddy to have something. . . . Ya'll oughta know how it

is, 'bout having something, 'cause y'all got something already. Y'all got land" (*Memphis*, 95).

Family issues also take a backseat to racial incidents in *The Road to Memphis*, but Taylor certainly doesn't minimize the Logans' reliance on family solidarity. For example, David Logan still plays an important role in his children's lives. When Cassie rather foolishly walks alone on the country road to the church, she is accosted by three white boys. Her father appears in time to save her from a potentially dangerous situation. As they walk back to the Great Faith Church, he explains that ever since she was an infant, he could usually sense when she was in trouble, when she needed him. "Always wanted to protect all my children," he says. "Figured, though, maybe you might be needing protection most" (*Memphis*, 104). Because this story extends beyond the community of Great Faith, other relatives provide the assistance David Logan would have provided at home. When friends of Stacey's and Cassie's get into trouble in Strawberry and eventually have to flee to Memphis, Cassie and Stacey rely on relatives in Jackson and on Uncle Hammer for assistance.

Cassie endures several harrowing experiences while on the road to Memphis, and her old fears of night men and racial violence resurface. Too upset to sleep, she seeks comfort in her memories of family, her home, and the land; for a time, those good thoughts allow her to relax enough to sleep. Their journey to Memphis is filled with rascals and tragedy. Clarence dies of a brain hemorrhage, Moe flees to Chicago, and Cassie has enough terrifying racial encounters to last her a lifetime. When it's over Cassie and Stacey return home once again to heal before going back out into the world. At home, they are comforted by their family, and in a scene familiar to the Logans, they kneel together in a circle in front of the fireplace, holding each other's hands as each member of the family prays for loved ones and friends.

Finally, Taylor borrows a device from *Roll of Thunder, Hear My Cry* to show how important family—or the lack of one—can be. In *Roll of Thunder*, Taylor juxtaposed T. J. Avery's family circumstances with the Logans; in *The Road to Memphis*, Jeremy Simms' terrible family situation is contrasted with the Logans.

Early in the novel, while talking about the difficulties he has had with his father over the years, Jeremy openly admires the father-son relationship David and Stacey Logan share. Much later in the novel, Jeremy's father, Charlie Simms, a hateful racist, discovers that Jeremy had helped Moe Turner escape from Strawberry after Moe had beaten Jeremy's cousins. In a scene filled with raw, frightful hate, "enough to arouse the devil" (*Memphis,* 275), Charlie Simms beats and then disowns Jeremy as Stacey and Cassie look on, horrified. Charlie Simms is the perfect antithesis to David Logan; no Logan would ever abuse his own kin the way Charlie Simms does. At the end of the novel, Jeremy appears on the Logans' porch to say farewell to Stacey and the Logans, and Taylor makes it clear that Jeremy's tragedies are not over yet. The reader is left to ponder how different Jeremy's life would have been if he had been fortunate enough to have been born into a family like the Logans instead of the Simms.

Family and Land in *The Well*

Taylor's most recent book, *The Well: David's Story,* returns to her familiar themes of the importance of family and land. A long drought has dried up all the wells around Great Faith, Mississippi, all the wells except for the one belonging to the Logans. This earlier generation of Logans is as noble as Cassie's family; its members willingly share their water with neighbors, black and white, including the obnoxious and ungrateful Simms. This batch of Logans follows the pattern established for the Logans in the previous books in many ways, including an absent father, in this case Paul Edward Logan who along with his two oldest sons is working away from home. The children miss their father dearly, but they understand that his work is necessary to keep their land. Even at their young ages, David and Hammer understand how important the land is to their family. When they get mixed up with Charlie Simms and face unfair consequences, Hammer initially resists the punishment but eventually swallows his pride rather than jeopardize the family and the land.

Family ties are equally important. Taylor makes clear how much Hammer and David miss their father—and how much their mother and the entire family suffer when he is gone. When their father is home, he takes time to teach his sons important lessons of life and does so without allowing them to escape the natural consequences of their actions. Their grandmother, Ma Rachel, also passes on family values, especially in the stories she tells of her own childhood, born into slavery. Her family story about the whipping her mother endured to preserve Ma Rachel's name shows the boys that family members are willing to make tremendous sacrifices in order to preserve important aspects of the family.

The brevity of *The Well* does not allow Taylor much room for development, but in her brief narrative, she does establish the Logan heritage: the Logan family loves one another and sticks together, and because the land is essential to their survival, the Logans will go to great lengths to protect their land and to retain ownership of it.

Family and Land in Taylor's Short Novels: The Gold Cadillac, The Friendship, Mississippi Bridge

Taylor's three short books, *The Gold Cadillac, The Friendship,* and *Mississippi Bridge,* continue, to varying degrees, her focus on family and land; however, none of these novellas is long enough to provide Taylor the space for a sustained narrative and a full development of family or land themes. *Mississippi Bridge* is the story of tragedy averted for some of the Logans' friends, and other than appearances by the close-knit Logan children, the book deals little or not at all with Taylor's familiar themes. Similarly, in *The Friendship* the Logan children merely observe an event that unfolds at the Wallace Store. In both of these books, the Logan children learn lessons about racism and human beings that reinforce what they've been taught at home, but other than that, these two books are concerned more with singular events than they are with Taylor's favorite two themes.

The Gold Cadillac stands out among Taylor's books to date because it is the only book she has written that is not about the Logans in Mississippi. Despite its departure from the pattern of her other Logan books, Taylor's familiar threads of family are woven throughout the narrative. She describes, lovingly, her parents and their relationship, her life surrounded by uncles and aunts, and her childhood in Toledo. She reveals the strength of the Taylor family in two ways: first, by the way her parents worked out their disagreement over the Cadillac, and second by the way the Taylors rely on one another for comfort and support when they encounter a racist policeman.

In addition to painting a truer picture of black families, a picture based on her own experience growing up in a nurturing, loving, supportive family, in her books Taylor has also succeeded in demonstrating just how essential land ownership was to the Logan family. Efforts to keep land and family intact provide the Logans with many opportunities to demonstrate their nobility and to grow together in cooperation and love. Their unity and determination ultimately help them to prevail over all their hardships, and more importantly, their actions provide inspiring examples of what families can be.

6. Learning about America: A Growing Awareness of Racism and Inequality

The steady undercurrent of racism stirs the water in all of Mildred D. Taylor's books. Often in her stories, it breaks through the surface to cause fear and tragedy; at other times, it remains submerged, ominously dormant for a time, creating tension because no one knows when it will suddenly drag another victim into its undertow of violence and discrimination. Parents of children who live near the ocean don't raise their children from infancy with terrifying stories of people dragged out to sea by a riptide and drowned. Gradually, as their children get older and begin spending more time in the water, swimming farther out from the beach, wise parents realize they must teach their children the dangers that coexist with the normally benign tides. Teaching young swimmers about riptides is, of course, only the first step; swimmers must also learn how to survive the undertow.

Part of raising children in a racist culture meant shielding them in their early youth from some of the more painful or dangerous facets of racism. For example, Taylor's father's and mother's families tried to keep their children away from the town because town life differed greatly from their rural life, and the chances were high that the children would face "other aspects of racism which the parents were not ready for them to face yet. They tried to protect the children."[1] Taylor's own parents, well-versed in the currents of a racist, discriminatory society, did not poison young Mildred's mind with stories of night men and violence and death. Instead, when she was young they surrounded her with loving, wise relatives, bathed her with love and attention, and taught her self-respect and pride in her family. These values came from a system her grandparents had taught to her father, uncles, and aunts and one that they in turn passed on to Taylor, her sister, and their cousins. It was a matter of "how to survive under this racist system and also how to keep one's own dignity and own self-respect" (Taylor Video).

But they could not—and knew they should not—shield her forever from the world in which they lived, a world that for the most part considered blacks to be inferior, a world that expended great effort to keep blacks apart from whites and to deprive black people of the basic rights white people enjoyed. Likewise, they knew they could not shield her from the fear, hate, and violence engendered by a racist society. Inevitably, for her own good, she would first have to learn about racism and then how to survive it.

Learning about Racism

Taylor had her first lessons about racism when she was perhaps seven or eight years old. As a young child, she always loved her family's regular trips to Mississippi, viewing the trip itself as a 20-hour picnic. Later, she realized that her mother packed food to take along in the car because after they left Ohio, they wouldn't be allowed to eat in "White Only" restaurants. She realized that they drove straight through because they wouldn't be allowed to stay in "White Only" hotels or motels along the way to Mississippi. She learned that the police stopped her father in the South not for speeding or any other traffic violation but for being a black man driving a nice new car. She saw the signs, "White Only, Colored Not Allowed" over restroom doors and drinking fountains. On her trips to Mississippi she learned much about her family and her heritage, but she also learned about racial discrimination in the South.

A few months before her tenth birthday, Taylor's father took her and her family on a trip to California. She knew it would be very different from their traditional trips to Mississippi and

During a stop in Nebraska on their trip to California, nine-year-old Taylor poses in front of her father's Oldsmobile.

assumed that among those differences would be less racial prejudice in the West. She was partially right; she saw no signs barring "Coloreds" from businesses, but because they were black, she and her family were denied service at some motels and restaurants on their way to California. On that trip, she was disappointed to learn that for black Americans second-class citizenship was not restricted to the South (*SAAS*, 273).

Her education about racism continued. When her family moved from their large duplex on the busy street in Toledo to a lovely, newly integrated neighborhood, she noticed many "For Sale" signs in the yards of many of the houses. When she asked her father why so many people wanted to sell such nice homes, he explained to her that when blacks moved into a neighborhood, whites moved out because they were afraid of blacks and were worried that with blacks in the area, property values would plummet. Her new neighborhood had an integrated school, and when she enrolled in the school in fifth grade, she learned firsthand what it was like to be a minority: she was one of only a handful of black students in the school; in sixth grade, she was the only black student in her class (*SAAS*, 273).

Academically, Taylor always did well in school, but her academic success couldn't prevent the isolation she felt because she was black. This alienation may have come less from the difference in skin color between Taylor and her white classmates than from the school curriculum, especially on the subject of history, that seemed to undermine all that she knew about blacks and their heritage. Blacks as portrayed in her school's history books and in the library books she read were not heroic, courageous, or admirable. In her acceptance speech for the *Boston Globe/Horn Book* Award, Taylor talked about this time in her life, a time when she learned that the white history of blacks in America contradicted the history she had learned from her family.

> During that year and the years that followed, classes devoted to the history of black people in the United States always caused me painful embarrassment. This was because history had not been presented truly, showing the accomplishments of blacks both in Africa and in this hemisphere. But, as it was, as the textbooks and the teachers presented the history, the indictment of slavery was also an indictment of the people who were enslaved—a people who, according to the texts, were docile and childlike, accepting their fate without once attempting to free themselves. To me this lackluster history of black people, totally devoid of any heroic or pride-building qualities, was as much a condemnation of myself as it was of my ancestors. I used to sit tensely waiting out those class hours trying to think of ways to

repudiate what the textbooks said, for I recognized that there was a terrible contradiction between what was in them and what I learned at home. (*Boston Globe,* 180)

Taylor later recalled that whenever her class studied the Civil War she wanted to miss school because those lessons inevitably included study of "the Negro," and she always felt demeaned by the ways the books presented "the Negro."

The school and textbook histories of blacks failed to inspire the pride Taylor always felt when she listened to her family's stories. In an effort to correct the misconceptions taught about blacks, she once shared with her classmates some of her inspiring family stories about the accomplishments of her grandparents and great-grandparents. Unfortunately, her attempt to correct history failed. Many of her classmates thought she had made up the stories, and some even laughed at her. Even her teacher didn't believe her. Everyone assumed that the history of blacks as portrayed in their textbooks was true (*SAAS,* 274). During this time Taylor continued to enjoy the stories told at family gatherings, but now she was more aware than ever before of the tales of racial encounters her father, uncles, and ancestors had endured. No longer shielded by her family, she was learning what she had to learn, that America was not the land of the free, at least not for blacks.

Taylor also learned about key events of the civil rights movement that occurred during her youth. The landmark Supreme Court ruling, *Brown* v. *Board of Education of Topeka,* which overturned the "separate but equal" regulations of segregated schools, was delivered when she was 11. She was almost 12 when young Emmet Till was murdered in Mississippi, and the national and black media widely publicized the crime and the trial. In December of the same year, Rosa Parks was arrested for refusing to give up her seat on a public bus, an event that led to the famous Montgomery bus boycott. The year Taylor started high school, 1957, was the same year that a handful of black students integrated Central High School in Little Rock, Arkansas. Taylor knew of these important events, of course, and she had personal experience with racial discrimination and prejudice, but she was unfamiliar with the open hostility that surrounded the civil rights events taking place in the South. Toledo seemed safe, far removed from the ugliness of what was happening in the South.

Learning from Personal Experience

One of Taylor's first encounters with the racial hostility she thought existed only in the South came during her first year of high school. That year, the students of Scott High School elected a black girl as the first homecoming queen in the history of the school and the city of Toledo. The election immediately polarized the school. Black and white students distanced themselves from one another, regarding the other group with caution; a black queen was hung in effigy; tension mounted as rumors spread that the girl might not be crowned homecoming queen, that there might be a black versus white rumble, that the homecoming game might be canceled, that some football players might boycott the game. The turmoil even drew TV coverage, and ministers in town came together to call for peace. In the end, the girl was crowned homecoming queen and tempers cooled, but the entire incident taught Taylor that racism was not restricted to the South (*SAAS,* 276). By the time Taylor graduated from high school, she no longer harbored any naive notions about racism and equality in the United States.

In accepting the Newbery Award, Mildred D. Taylor expressed her desire to continue the Logan family saga in a way that would present a black child's "hopes and fears from childhood innocence to awareness to bitterness and disillusionment" ("Newbery," 407). Perhaps one of the strongest autobiographical details in Taylor's books is the parallel between Taylor's own growing awareness of racism and that of Cassie Logan. Like Taylor, Cassie grew up in a loving, healthy, proud family that was able to protect Cassie from much of the ugliness of the world outside her home. But in Taylor's books, Cassie and Taylor's other two narrators, David Logan and Jeremy Simms, learn about racism from their direct experience. In many respects, nearly all of Taylor's books might be categorized as *bildungsroman,* novels of education, because in her books her main characters move away from childhood notions about how people should and do act and learn often painful lessons of the real world.

Cassie's Lessons

In *Song of the Trees* Cassie leads an almost idyllic life. Her mother and grandmother love and care for her; her brothers are loveable and kind; her father is brave and trustworthy. She spends many hours in the forest on her family's property, reveling in the beauty of nature and especially her trees. When her father confronts Mr. Andersen, she sees for perhaps the first time the powerful and potentially deadly nature of racism. Her father knows that only if he's willing to risk his life and the lives of Andersen and his cutting crew will he be able to save the forest. Andersen backs down, but not without threatening David Logan. At the end of the story, Cassie sees her father shaken by the incident while all around her lie the dead trees, victims of a white man's greed. This incident is Cassie's introduction to interracial conflict in her community.

Cassie's next encounter with racism comes about a year later and is reported in *The Friendship.* This encounter is similar to the one in *Song of the Trees* in that Cassie is not the direct victim of racism; she observes a racist event as it unfolds, but even as an observer, she is deeply affected by it. Cassie sees for the first time the irrationality and violence that accompany racism in the South. She is initially surprised that calling a white man by his first name is even an issue, but she is stunned when she watches the angry reaction of the other white men in the Wallace Store who push Wallace into taking action against Mr. Tom Bee. A review in the *Wilson Library Bulletin* noted that the power of the story will have perhaps as great an impact on readers as it did on Cassie Logan. "No one will be left unaffected by its quiet terror; no one can ask 'So what's the big deal?' The humiliation, the injustice, but above all the quiet determination, courage, and pride of Mr. Tom Bee will speak to all children of where we have been, where we are today, and just how far we have to go to preserve and perpetuate the heritage of this old man's pride and feelings of self-worth."[2] After witnessing her first act of racial violence and its accompanying humiliation and injustice, Cassie is somewhat better prepared for other racist events she will observe and experience later in her life.

Cassie's understanding of racism grows considerably in *Roll of Thunder, Hear My Cry,* a novel for which critic David Rees praised Taylor for coming "closer than anyone else to giving us a really good novel about racial prejudice."[3] Initially, Cassie is aware of the subtle discrimination she and her brothers endure: walking instead of riding a school bus; attending a ramshackle, underfunded school; using textbooks that have been discarded by the white school. She learns of racial violence when she hears from T. J. Avery that some white men had burned three men from the Berry family, but the vague secondhand report has little impact on her.

Racism becomes more personal for her when she and her brothers are run off the road by the white school bus. Later, she hears about—and sees—the notorious night men on the prowl, then hears that Sam Tatum has been tarred and feathered by them. The violent results of racism become real to Cassie when her mother takes her and her brothers to visit Mr. Berry, a man burned beyond recognition, barely clinging to life. Mary Logan explains to her children that the Wallaces burned Mr. Berry and his two nephews and that the Wallace Store is a dangerous place for black children. It was a lesson Cassie wouldn't forget.

Not much later, Cassie has her most painful and personal lesson about racism to date. On Cassie's first-ever trip to Strawberry, she is kept waiting by Mr. Barnett, the white storekeeper, because of the steady stream of white customers whom he serves first. When Cassie angrily complains about his poor service, she's insulted and humiliated by him and rescued by Stacey before the situation becomes explosive. Outside the store, she bumps into Lillian Jean Simms, and to her great shame is forced, first by Lillian Jean, then by her father, Charlie Simms, to apologize. The humiliation is almost more than Cassie can bear, and when she tells her mother about the experience, Mary Logan says, "Baby, you had to grow up a little today" (*Thunder,* 126) and explains to Cassie the basis of the discriminatory society in which they live. Fair-minded Cassie can barely comprehend the irrationality of racism, even as it's explained by her mother. For Cassie the day, filled with painful lessons about discrimination and racism, was the cruelest of her life. In a video interview, Taylor explains the impact this scene had on her protagonist: "Cassie and her brother hadn't had to face this yet because they weren't of that age—but Cassie does go into Strawberry and she does learn a harsh truth. Because her parents have tried to protect her, it comes as a jolt to her when she realizes that once again black people are not considered equal to whites"(Taylor Video).

Harder Lessons

Cassie doesn't know that these events are only the beginning of her education about racism in Mississippi. Later in *Roll of Thunder* Cassie's father teaches her why blacks can't be friends with white folks, even white folks as seemingly innocuous as Jeremy Simms. She then witnesses the decline and tragic fall of T. J. after he takes up with two older white boys. Near the novel's end, she watches as T. J. is brutally beaten by a white lynch mob and later learns that her father has set fire to part of his crop in order to distract the mob and save T. J.'s life. She will never forget the events of that night; they have permanently changed her life and her world view. Cassie matures in many ways in *Roll of Thunder,* but among her most lasting lessons are those that teach her that the world outside her home is not always a friendly or safe place and even though her own strong self-image makes her certain that, "Ah, shoot! White ain't nothin'!" (*Thunder,* 127), in the segregated South of the 1930s, white was indeed something whether she liked it or not.

Cassie's growing awareness of racism continues in *Let the Circle Be Unbroken.* While in Strawberry for the murder trial of T. J.

Avery, she encounters formal segregation for the first time. At the court house, she sees that the courtroom has segregated seating, with most seats reserved for whites and only a single bench in a corner of the room for blacks. Before the trial, her brothers unknowingly use the "Whites Only" toilet and Cassie drinks from a "Whites Only" drinking fountain. Luckily, Jeremy Simms helps them cover their potentially dangerous error, but he infuriates Cassie by tearing her away from the drinking fountain. He and Stacey try to explain what she and her brothers have done wrong, but as with her other lessons on racism, this lesson on segregation makes no sense to her: "There was so much to learn, too much of it bad. Water was water, a toilet a toilet. Were people crazy?" (*Circle,* 59).

That is only the beginning of the craziness Cassie witnesses that day. T. J.'s trial completes his tragic downfall, and by watching how unfairly the white legal system persecutes a poor black victim, Cassie learns that as a young black person, she is guaranteed little protection outside her family. Her first introduction to the discriminatory Mississippi legal system comes when Mr. Jamison explains to Cassie and Stacey that there would not be any black jurors at the trial because juries were selected from voter rolls, and no blacks were registered to vote. At the trial itself, Cassie watches as Mr. Jamison produces irrefutable evidence to exonerate T. J. of any involvement in the murder of Mr. Barnett, but the all-white jury ignores the evidence and convicts T. J. anyway because he is black. T. J.'s trial teaches Cassie a lesson about racism in America similar to the lesson Taylor herself probably learned when she read about Emmett Till's murder and the mockery of a trial held for his murderers. Cassie learns that even with a willing, wise, and white benefactor like Mr. Jamison, young blacks really don't have any legal protection in Mississippi.

Institutional Racism

In addition to finding out something about the white legal system, Cassie also learns that the larger system of white governance is prejudiced against blacks. The Logan family and all of their sharecropping neighbors have suffered incredible economic hardship because of the federal government's agricultural programs that require farmers to destroy a significant portion of their crops. The promised government compensation for the lost crops is siphoned off by the white landowners, and the poor black farmers and sharecroppers are powerless to do anything about it. At about the same time an elderly friend of the Logans, Mrs. Lee Annie Lees, decides she wants to register to vote. By helping Mrs. Lee Annie prepare for the white-imposed "literacy test," Cassie learns about the hypocritical Mississippi constitution that rather than protect the rights of black citizens limits their rights. Despite the warnings of friends and family, Mrs. Lee Annie finally goes to the courthouse to attempt to register. Cassie wants to go, but her mother, knowing that the experience may be ugly or dangerous, is reluctant to allow Cassie to join them. Her father, however, points out that Cassie needs to learn about the discriminatory society in which she lives: "This thing she's wanting to do, it could be something she *needs* to see" (*Circle,* 333). Mrs. Lee Annie isn't allowed to register, of course, and her attempt is used as a catalyst to incite mob violence in Strawberry. This experience helps Cassie see how the systematic disenfranchisement of black voters has kept blacks without any political power and how determined whites are to maintain the status quo.

The oppressive white power structure causes great personal suffering and loss to Cassie and her family. The economic adversity of the Depression, made worse by the government's programs and local white corruption, have put the Logan land at risk. The family must earn enough cash each year to pay the taxes and the mortgage. Hoping to add to the family income, Stacey runs away from home to join an itinerant sugar cane cutting crew. What Stacey doesn't realize, however, is that white men are taking advantage of ignorant black youths who sign on to cane crews for the promise of good wages. The cane crews are little more than slave labor, and the boys live and work under terrible conditions with no promise of pay or freedom. Cassie observes the great pain Stacey's absence causes the family, including tension between her parents, and when he is finally rescued, she is stunned by the harrowing tales he shares of his experiences in the cane fields. Stacey's experience teaches Cassie that most whites cannot be trusted, that greedy white men are always willing to exploit blacks.

A convergence of events provides Cassie with a more personal introduction to the complications of interracial relationships. Jacey Peters, a black girl about Stacey's age, has drawn the attention of white Stuart Granger, and more than once, Cassie sees Jacey basking in Stuart's attention despite the warnings of many who know her. Jeremy Simms, the only white friend of Cassie and Stacey, as a token of his friendship gives each of them his photograph. And Mary Logan's cousin Bud Rankin, who has married a white woman and fathered a mixed-race daughter, appears in Great Faith. After each one of these events, Uncle Hammer explains to Cassie, not always nicely, how dangerous it is for blacks to mix with whites. It's a lesson Cassie will never forgot, a lesson later and more gently reinforced by her father, who tells her that white men have been using black women for centuries, and "it's a mighty hurting thing . . . mighty hurting" (*Circle,* 179). In addition to the lectures from her father and uncle, Cassie sees the fallout from black and white relations: Jacey Peters becomes pregnant by Stuart Granger; Cousin Bud's wife leaves him; Jeremy is beaten and then disowned by his father for befriending blacks; Bud's daughter, Suzella, is unsure of her identity, and her presence in Great Faith draws the wrath of white men. By the end of this novel, Cassie has learned by lecture and by experience that in the place and times in which she lives, whites and blacks cannot live together happily.

In *The Road to Memphis,* the education of Cassie, now 17, takes a darker turn. The racist events in this novel are both more personal and more horrible than those in any of the previous novels, and these experiences seem to complete Cassie's education. Though by now Cassie has learned plenty about racism, it strikes closer than ever to her and to people she cares about. Her friends Harris Mitchum and Moe Turner are humiliated and hurt by racists; Cassie is nearly molested by three white boys on her way back to the Great Faith Church; on the way to Memphis, she is verbally abused and nearly beaten for trying to use a "Whites

Only" restroom; their friend Clarence dies because he is refused treatment at a white hospital; Moe must live in exile because he has beaten some white men; Jeremy Simms is brutally abused by his father for befriending blacks. The culmination of these events and their impact on her cause Cassie at one point to complain about her friends serving in the segregated military, and about all the events in the novel, "It's not right. It's not right" (*Memphis*, 234). Cassie has learned that racism and its effects are neither fair nor right, but she has also learned that there is little she can do about them. Whites have too much power, too much control, too much experience in manipulating and taking advantage of blacks. But in addition to learning about racism, Cassie has learned how to survive it as well. Her father taught her the importance of self-respect, courage, and intelligence in dealing with the oppressive majority. Her encounters with Solomon Bradley, a successful black lawyer and activist, complement the lessons taught by her father. Bradley has become successful not because he is violent or strong but because he is smart. His example coupled with her father's example and teachings help Cassie realize that despite the discriminatory hurdles she will inevitably face, she really can become whatever she sets her mind to become. When Cassie reflects on the events of the novel, she says, "So much had changed" (*Memphis*, 288). She also realizes that much from her childhood has been lost and will never be regained. *The Road to Memphis* completes Cassie's education; she has learned what she needs to learn in order to survive, perhaps even thrive, in a racist society.

Innocence and Disillusionment

Three other books—the novellas *The Gold Cadillac, Mississippi Bridge,* and *The Well*—do not feature Cassie Logan as narrator but do, as her other books have, focus on a child's growth from innocence to awareness to disillusionment. *The Gold Cadillac* is an autobiographical story of a trip Taylor's family made from Ohio to Mississippi in a brand new car her father had purchased.

Along the way, he is harassed and eventually arrested, and 'lois, the narrator, is terrified of what might happen to her father and to her family. Though it is a very brief story, the *New York Times Book Review* described it as "a personal, poignant look at a black child's first experience with institutional racism" (Wesley, 37). The young 'lois learns that even in a strong, loving, middle-class family, she and those she loves remain at risk because they are black.

In *Mississippi Bridge,* young Jeremy Simms observes several ironies of racism. In the Wallace store, he watches Mr. Wallace deny the black woman Rudine permission to try on a hat without first buying it, though minutes later Mr. Wallace allows the white Miz Hattie to try it on. Jeremy also sees his unemployed tenant farming father and older brothers belittle Josias Williams for saying he has found a job. When the bus arrives a little later, all the blacks, including Josias, are made to get off the bus to make room for white passengers. Minutes later when the bus crashes off the bridge and into a flooding river, Jeremy helps Josias pull bodies from the wreckage. Ironically, segregated busing saved the lives of the black characters in this story at the expense of white characters. In *Twentieth-Century Young Adult Writers,* Karen Patricia Smith writes that "Taylor's irony seems less a contrivance of fate than a startling portrayal of Old Testament justice, enacting an event designed to exact payment for all of the injustices experienced in past stories, and in the past, collectively."[4] The lesson is not lost on young Jeremy.

David Logan, Cassie's father, as the 10-year-old narrator of *The Well,* learns some of the same lessons he will one day pass on to Cassie. When members of the Simms family come to draw water from the Logan well, Hammer stands up to their bullying but his stubbornness leads to trouble for David and Hammer. As David said, "White folks could say or do what they wanted, just because they ruled things; because just one word out of them against a black person—man or woman, or even a child—and that black man or that black woman or that child could be hanging from a tree, even just for mouthing off" (*Well,* 12). Later David recoils at the ugliness of the word "nigger;" he hears the sad story of his grandmother, Rachel, and how her mother's owners tried to steal her name; and he learns about racism from his father, himself a son of a white man and a slave woman. These lessons combine with the central action of the plot, the racist and cruel actions of Charlie Simms and his family, to give David Logan the same insight and experience Cassie Logan receives in most of Taylor's other books: racism is evil, unfair, and cruel; racists are inhuman; blacks can overcome racism by relying on their intelligence instead of violence.

In her acceptance speech for the ALAN Award, Taylor repeated what she has said before about her books: her goal has been to present a "true picture" of the lives of blacks in America based on her own experiences and those of her family. "In all of the books," she said, "I have recounted not only the joy of growing up in a large and supportive family, but my own feelings of being faced with segregation and bigotry. Writing these feelings was never easy, but when my first books were published, those feelings and the history I presented were understood. Yes, people would say. We remember how it was" (*ALAN,* 3). The characters in her stories learn about bigotry and segregation and how to survive in a racist society, and through Taylor's stories, readers—black and white—can learn those same lessons.

7. Balancing Reality and Hope

After the biblical character Job has suffered all kinds of loss and hardships, he laments in one part of his Old Testament story, "My days are swifter than a weaver's shuttle, and are spent without hope" (Job 7:6). It is natural for people who endure trials and suffering to become bitter, to give up hope even though they usually realize that hope is essential for survival. And because it is natural for human beings to give up hope in the face of overwhelming odds, society admires those who don't succumb, those who maintain their pride and dignity—their humanity—through difficult experiences that would make most people "curse God, and die" (Job 2:9). Survivors of the Nazi Holocaust, for example, often cited their refusal to surrender hope as a key to their survival of the horrors of the death camps; their courage and optimism in such terrifying and hopeless circumstances are inspiring to all people.

The families of Mildred D. Taylor, both her actual and her fictional families, suffered more than enough at the hands of racists to become justifiably bitter and angry, but Taylor's families would not allow themselves to sink to the level of their tormentors. The Taylors and the Logans maintained their self-respect and refused to let their spirits be broken by the discriminatory society in which they lived. Taylor herself grew up in the early days of the civil rights movement, reading about, observing, or experiencing all manner of inequities and cruelties dealt to blacks. As a graduate student at the University of Colorado, she was active in the Black Student Alliance, which in the 1960s worked to establish black pride and to overcome discrimination. She grew up listening to stories of how her father and other relatives suffered the inequities of racism. Based on her experience and the experiences of her family and friends, Taylor has plenty of reasons to be bitter and angry about how her family and her race have been treated in their own country. And if she were bitter, it is very likely that her bitterness would find its way into her stories. The fact that the Logan stories are laced with hope suggests that Taylor herself has managed to do what her family and characters have done: to see racism for what it is and to condemn it but to do so without bitterness.

Establishing a Balance

In her books Taylor pulls no punches in her presentation of racism. Readers share with the Logans the sadness, pain, frustration, and rage they feel as they confront discrimination, segregation, and hatred. Fortunately, however, Taylor balances the realities of racism with hope, and by doing so enables her stories to soar above mere anti-racist sermons or harangues. Her portrayal of the Logans not as victims but as survivors allows Taylor to deal honestly and accurately with the painful conflicts of racism without making her stories completely hopeless. Karen Patricia Smith's article, "A Chronicle of Family Honor: Balancing Rage and Triumph in the Novels of Mildred D. Taylor" is about this balance of realism and optimism in Taylor's books. Smith says, "One of the unique aspects of Taylor's work is her focus upon a strong, upwardly mobile family unit which consistently, and also realistically, manages to meet 'head-on' the social challenges of racism and disenfranchisement."[1] Taylor's books are often praised for their realistic portrayal of racism, but it is the hopeful, even optimistic tone of her stories that contributes to their popularity. Achieving this tone came as the result of a conscious effort by Taylor to maintain a balance between realism and hope in her stories. In a video interview, she explains, "One of the things I've tried to do in all the Logan books . . . was to balance all the books with the good times because [the Logans], of course, were living in a racist society, they were living under segregation, but out in the rural areas [racism] was not a day-to-day thing that they were experiencing. They many times did have so many good aspects to their lives" (Taylor Video).

Indeed, it is the "good aspects" of the Logan stories that make them memorable and inspiring. One critic praised Taylor for her ability to blend unpleasant aspects of history with the nobility of family. She wrote that Taylor's books "bring alive a fragment of the history of black life in the Deep South for a generation that doesn't know much about it except, at best, secondhand. And, though Cassie Logan, her family and friends undergo a seemingly endless series of cruel trials at the hands of their white neighbors, Ms. Taylor has better news for us—she paints an appealingly detailed picture of the warm family relations and the embracing communal spirit to remind us that black life, day to day, however troubled, is not the disaster it looks like when it is simplified by sociology" (Brown, 48). The "better news" of Taylor's books effectively offsets the realistic and powerful presentation of racism that might otherwise overwhelm her readers and undermine the impact of her stories.

Of course, given their setting, there is plenty of bad news in Taylor's stories. Though critics frequently praise the strong family values and the realistic historical details in her books, it would be inaccurate to say that her books are only historical, family stories. The fruits of racism—discrimination, segregation, abuse—are essential threads in the fabric of all of Taylor's narratives. The lives of the Logans and their friends are unavoidably shaped by the hostile racist environment, and the conditions in which they live require them to spend inordinate amounts of time fighting simply to survive. The racial conflicts in Taylor's stories are not mere side issues; they play important roles in the narratives by providing the Logans a variety of imposing challenges to overcome. The Logans' efforts to triumph over these challenges reveal their nobility, strength of character, and good sense.

The bad news appears in many forms in Taylor's books. One type, institutional abuse, is typified by the monopoly of the Wallace Store, the oppression of sharecroppers, the poorly funded Great Faith School, T. J.'s trial and subsequent murder conviction, the unfair New Deal agricultural programs that robbed the Logans of crops and cash, the disenfranchisement of black voters in general and Mrs. Lee Annie Lees in particular, the organized pressure to shut down attempts to establish a farmers union, segregated buses and other public facilities, the lack of defense industry jobs for blacks, and other overt and subtle Jim Crow practices. The institutional abuse, though at times cruel, usually has a more indirect effect on the Logans; it may put their property or livelihood at risk, but usually it causes more annoyance or frustration than direct physical threat.

The more painful types of racial conflict come from individual abuse, the misuse of the authority over blacks to abuse them personally, and there are many examples in Taylor's books: the whipping young David and Hammer get from their mother because of Charlie Simms, veiled or blatant threats against the Logans from a variety of white characters, Mr. Granger's machinations to steal the Logan land, marauding night men, the lynch mob that assaults T. J., the Wallaces' attack on David Logan, Stuart Granger's attentions to Suzella and the later humiliation of Cousin Bud, Stacey's forced labor in the cane fields, the Aames brothers abusing Moe and Clarence, the verbal abuse and the pursuit on the road to Memphis, and other direct assaults on black characters. These painful and ugly events could easily overshadow Taylor's stories, but she skillfully frames them in the context of a larger story, not to de-emphasize them but to keep them in perspective. Her judicious use of these racial events in her stories is key to the balance between realism and hope and reveals Taylor's acute awareness of the importance of a balanced narrative.

Using Conflict to Accomplish a Higher Purpose

Taylor's balance between reality and hope does not suggest that she is soft on racism. Her characters often express righteous and justified indignation at the inequities they face, an indignation shared by readers. Her balance does, however, allow her to accomplish a higher purpose as described in an article by Karen Patricia Smith, which asserts that Taylor's positive focus on the benefits of a nuclear family, ambition, and hard work is one of the strengths of the Logan books. That focus, however, "does not mean that the hardships endured by a person of color should be submerged within a sea of optimism and certainly, Taylor does not do this. It also does not mean that one will not, or should not be entitled to experience a certain rage at injustices rendered. But what it does mean is that a youthful and also adult audience needs (and indeed *deserves*) to have the opportunity to see the good that can come of *not giving up and not giving in;* that there is the possibility of *triumph* at the end of adversity" (Smith, 249). The Logans know, despite the heaps of adversity they constantly face, that not only will they survive, they will thrive. Their innate faith in themselves and their optimism about the future work together to effectively counter the depressing aspects of their stories and contribute in a large way to the upbeat tenor of all of Taylor's books. Smith goes on to suggest that the very balance Taylor seems to understand so well as a storyteller is also evident as a key to survival for the Logan family: "Balance of a spiritual, social, economic, and political nature, in as much as the key players are able to 'juggle' the internal mechanisms of each of the components (rather than one element against another), may be seen to be the key to the survival of the Logan family"(Smith, 249). For example, if the Logans became obsessed with the inequities of their lives or the bad breaks that come their way, they might easily take the less cautious route and retaliate with violence or the less heroic route and "curse God, and die." Their healthy perspective keeps them afloat when nothing else could, and perhaps more importantly, it reminds readers that unfortunate circumstances do not necessarily negate the possibility of a good life.

The positive qualities of the Logan family are essential for their survival, but these qualities also effectively counterbalance the bad news of racism that permeates Taylor's books. By focusing her narratives on the Logans' efforts to survive instead of on their woes, she tips the readers' main attention away from the cruelty and inherent evil of racism to the personal qualities one must have to overcome adversities as monumental as systematic discrimination and oppression. For example, *Roll of Thunder*'s memorable scene of Cassie's encounter at the Barnett Store in Strawberry, her first direct experience with racism, is effectively counterbalanced by a more effective and lasting scene where Cassie's mother consoles her and teaches her about living in a racist society. Mary concludes their conversation by reminding Cassie, "we have no choice of what color we're born or who our parents are or whether we're rich or poor. What we do have is some choice over what we make of our lives once we're here" (*Thunder,* 129). Throughout Taylor's novels, Cassie returns often to the nurturing strength of her family to sustain her in difficult times.

The importance of friendship is also used to counterbalance the negative aspects of racism in the lives of the Logans and in Taylor's books. Hypocritical T. J. Avery often annoys the Logan children, but Stacey values him as a friend and along with Cassie ultimately benefits from his efforts to stand by T. J. through hard times. Jeremy Simms, a persistent and enigmatic friend, shows unconditional love for his Logan friends despite their occasional rebuffs. His willingness to sacrifice his connections with his own family to help Moe escape demonstrate his unwavering commitment and loyalty to Stacey and Cassie. Wordell Lees' vigil during Cassie's illness in *Let the Circle Be Unbroken* and the faithful support of Mr. Wade Jamison in several of the Logan stories reinforce both the pleasure and necessity of friendship. These examples of friendship demonstrate that good friends can be found even in hellish circumstances, and that in such circumstances, friends play a vital role in one's survival.

Because faith is such an essential part of her family, Taylor's books contain an undefined spirituality, a religious faith that both sustains the Logans through their trials and prevents them from becoming too caught up in the worldly issues of economics, materialism, and racism. Reverend Gabson and his Great Faith

Church are central figures in Taylor's three Logan novels, and though Cassie often grows tired of Reverend Gabson's long and powerful sermons, it is clear that the church plays an essential role in the community and in the Logans' lives. Whether or not Reverend Gabson ever preached from Paul's epistle to the Corinthians about "faith, hope, and charity," the Logans certainly are living examples of these Christian qualities. The Logans themselves benefit from their own Christian attitudes, but so do the neighbors who often partake of the Logans' generosity and kindness. In addition to being churchgoing folks, the Logans often pray together as a family at home, and their prayers help to sustain them in times of peril, worry, or tragedy. The spiritual principles and practices of the Logans help them to weather the various storms of conflict in Taylor's books and once again counterbalance the bleaker aspects of her stories.

Taylor also overcomes the bleakness of racism in her stories by refusing to allow her characters to be willing or meek victims. The lyrics of a song that Taylor wrote for her first novel reflect an attitude of resilience and resistance:

> Roll of thunder
> hear my cry
> Over the water
> bye and bye
> Ole man comin'
> down the line
> Whip in hand to
> beat me down
> But I *ain't*
> gonna let him
> Turn me 'round.

This attitude of determined resistance to oppression resonates throughout Taylor's books, in which black resistance to racism takes many forms. David and Mary Logan often remind their children of the pride they have in their family and their race, and Mary teaches her children and her students a truer history of blacks in America than they receive from their schoolbooks. But perhaps the actions of David and Mary Logan speak louder than their words. They refuse to accept inequality and do whatever they can to resist racial discrimination. In *Roll of Thunder,* for example, even though they put their family and their land at risk, the Logans organize and lead the boycott of the Wallace Store. Possessing the same pluck and resilience as their parents, Stacey and Cassie resist in their own ways: Stacey helps the children disable the white school bus, Cassie finds a safe way to put Lillian Jean Simms in her place. In *Let the Circle Be Unbroken,* Cassie tutors Mrs. Lee Annie for the voter literacy test, and David Logan gives tacit support to the fledgling farmer's union. In *The Road to Memphis,* Cassie sees a remarkable example of resistance at a level previously unimaginable to her: Solomon Bradley owns and operates a black newspaper and uses his legal training to combat unfair treatment of blacks. The assorted resistance efforts against racism Taylor presents in her books help the Logans become more than victims, and it gives the Logans and Taylor's readers hope that eventually the courageous efforts of such people will one day eliminate intolerance and prejudice.

One of the essential ingredients in the oppressive Jim Crow society of the South was the limits on education. As long as blacks remained uneducated, they could be more easily "kept in their place." For poor blacks in the South, the myriad obstacles to decent education became discouraging, making it seem to some that they had no hope of escaping the dire circumstances in which they lived. But to readers of the Logan stories, the opportunity for advancement through education never seems hopeless because the Logans value common sense and learning. Several scenes in Taylor's books show Cassie or Stacey receiving a lecture from David or Hammer Logan about the importance of "using your head." And common sense tells them that education is worth sacrificing for. The children make the daily long walk to school even though they might be needed in the fields. Mary Logan is, of course, a teacher, and even after she loses her job at Great Faith School, she continues to teach her children and others at home. At night, the Logan children do their homework and read, often joining their parents. Books are mentioned in many of the Logan stories, often as prized Christmas gifts. When she is older, Cassie moves to Jackson to attend high school in order to have a better education, and her conversations with Solomon Bradley reveal her plans to attend college and perhaps become a lawyer. Taylor and the Logans know that there is hope as long as there is learning, and readers seeing the Logans' emphasis on education know that despite the racist obstacles, the Logan children will eventually realize their potential.

As mentioned above, Taylor does not allow the pall of racism to overshadow the "good aspects" of the lives of the Logans. From her very first book, she has included warm, loving family scenes: the children doing homework at night, the family reading together, the family working in the fields together, the children playing together, family gatherings and holiday celebrations, the family kneeling together in a circle to pray, quiet one-on-one talks between Cassie and one of her parents. Much as some authors use "comic relief" to vent tension from their stories, Taylor scatters these family scenes throughout her stories to buffer the intense and painful scenes of racial antagonism and violence. In addition to the family scenes, another good aspect of the Logans' life in rural Mississippi is food. Taylor often describes family meals in such succulent detail that readers are left with their mouths watering. When the Logans are enjoying a fine meal, it is hard to remember much about the suffering they have endured. Similarly, the vivid description of the land around Great Faith, Mississippi, creates a setting antithetical to the racist ugliness that resides within it. Cassie's affectionate verbal portraits of nature in various seasons of the year evoke a pleasant nostalgia; it is hard to imagine that anything bad could take place in it.

The Controversy of Realism

It is ironic that despite Taylor's consistent efforts to temper her painful representation of racism by balancing it with hope, some adults feel that Taylor's stories go too far in their realism, that many of the details in her stories are harmful to children. Taylor herself has often acknowledged the personal pain she endures when reliving stories of segregation and bigotry in order to write her books, but she continues writing her stories because of her deeply-felt commitment to her family's legacy. She also believes that today's youth and many of their teachers and parents have little understanding of the racism that was once standard in America and that her stories might help them gain an appreciation for what blacks once endured and have labored to overcome. Unfortunately, some people have missed her message and have been unable to see the balance in her stories. For some, perhaps especially for those who believe that anything unpleasant, even if it is true, should not be a subject for young adult books, balance is not enough. Instead, they see only harm in her books. In her acceptance speech for the ALAN Award, Taylor talked about the recent reaction to her work:

> I have recounted events that were painful to write and painful to be read, but I had hoped they brought more understanding. Now, however, there are those who think that perhaps my recountings are too painful and there are those who seek to remove books such as mine from school reading lists. There are some who say the books should be removed because the "N" word is used. There are some who say such events as described in my books and books by others did not happen. There are those who do not want to remember the past or who do not want their children to know the past and who would whitewash history, and these sentiments are not only from whites. (*ALAN,* 3)

It is surprising to think that anyone could object to any of Taylor's stories, but there have been some recent challenges to her books. In one state, a Hispanic father petitioned the school board to remove *The Well* from the school curriculum because it uses the word "nigger." When a black mother in another state protested her son's reading *Roll of Thunder, Hear My Cry* because she thought the book was too negative and because he was the only black student in the class, the school responded by making the boy sit in the hall while the class read. A black church in a northern state questioned whether or not children of church members should read *Roll of Thunder* in school. These objections bother Taylor because these adults have missed or misread the intentions of her stories. In her defense, Taylor says, "I am hurt that any child would ever be hurt by my words. As a parent I understand not wanting a child to hear painful words, but as a parent I do not understand not wanting a child to learn about a history that is part of America, a history about a family representing millions of families that are strong and loving and who remain united and strong, despite the obstacles they face" (*ALAN*, 3).

Taylor continues to write the history of the Logans, the story of how one family's unity and courage help its members survive racism. She acknowledges that these stories will offend people who insist on political correctness: "there will be some who will be offended, but as we all know, racism is offensive. It is not polite, and it is full of pain" (*ALAN*, 3). Unfortunately, the pain is part of the history, and if Taylor were to minimize the pain or unpleasantness concomitant with racism, she would be dishonest to herself and to the people whose stories she is telling. Taylor also feels very strongly that her family history and the larger history of blacks in America must be preserved. Lessons can be learned from reading about the nobility of their struggle and from reading about the abuses they suffered. She fears that if these stories are not told, people will forget the pains racism inflicted on so many people, and once people forget, the mistakes of history are likely to be repeated. Readers can be sure, however, that her stories will, as her previous stories have, maintain a balance between reality and hope, a balance that careful readers certainly will not miss.

Mildred D. Taylor's books about the Logan family reflect the bittersweet mix of American history. In the two centuries since declaring its independence, America has done many things to be proud of and many things to be ashamed of. Dwelling exclusively on one or the other, the bad or the good, would create an unbalanced view of this country's history. Some of the most valuable lessons to be learned from American history come from examining how Americans have confronted that bad side, from studying how they have grown because of their faults and conflicts, from determining if they were able to turn the bad into good. It is true that Taylor's stories focus on one very bad aspect of American history, but rather than condemn America for its racist history, her stories celebrate the nobility of Americans—black and white—who were able to rise above the racist culture. What could possibly be more inspiring, more positive, or more hopeful?

Appendix A
Civil Rights Amendments to
the U.S. Constitution

Amendment XIII to the U.S. Constitution

Section 1. Neither slavery nor involuntary servitude, except as a punishment for crime whereof the party shall have been duly convicted, shall exist within the United States, or any place subject to their jurisdiction.

Section 2. Congress shall have power to enforce this article by appropriate legislation.

Amendment XIV to the U.S. Constitution

Section 1. All persons born or naturalized in the United States, and subject to the jurisdiction thereof, are citizens of the United States and of the State wherein they reside. No State shall make or enforce any law which shall abridge the privileges or immunities of citizens of the United States; nor shall any State deprive any person of life, liberty, or property, without due process of law; nor deny to any person within its jurisdiction the equal protection of the laws.

Section 2. Representatives shall be apportioned among the several States according to their respective numbers, counting the whole number of persons in each State, excluding Indians not taxed. But when the right to vote at any election for the choice of electors for President and Vice-President of the United States, Representatives in Congress, the Executive and Judicial officers of a State, or the members of the Legislature thereof, is denied to any of the male inhabitants of such State, being twenty-one years of age, and citizens of the United States, or in any way abridged, except for participation in rebellion, or other crime, the basis of representation therein shall be reduced in the proportion which the number of such male citizens shall bear to the whole number of male citizens twenty-one years of age in such State.

Section 3. No person shall be a Senator or Representative in Congress, or elector of President and Vice President, or hold any office, civil or military, under the United States, or under any State, who, having previously taken an oath, as a member of Congress, or as an officer of the United States, or as a member of any State legislature, or as an executive or judicial officer of any State, to support the Constitution of the United States, shall have engaged in insurrection or rebellion against the same, or given aid or comfort to the enemies thereof. But Congress may by a vote of two-thirds of each House, remove such disability.

Section 4. The validity of the public debt of the United States, authorized by law, including debts incurred for payment of pensions and bounties for services in suppressing insurrection or rebellion, shall not be questioned. But neither the United States nor any State shall assume or pay any debt or obligation incurred in aid of insurrection or rebellion against the United States, or any claim for the loss or emancipation of any slave; but all such debts, obligations and claims shall be held illegal and void.

Section 5. The Congress shall have power to enforce, by appropriate legislation, the provisions of this article.

Amendment XV to the U.S. Constitution
Section 1. The right of citizens of the United States to vote shall not be denied or abridged by the United States or by any State on account of race, color, or previous condition of servitude.

Section 2. The Congress shall have power to enforce this article by appropriate legislation.

Appendix B
Awards Won by Mildred D. Taylor

Song of the Trees (1975)
Council on Interracial Books for Children Award
New York Times Outstanding Book of the Year
Coretta Scott King Honor Book
Jane Addams Honor Book

Roll of Thunder, Hear My Cry (1976)
Newbery Award
National Book Award finalist
ALA Notable Book
Notable Children's Trade Books in the Field of Social Studies
American Book Award
Young Reader's Choice
Boston Globe/Horn Book Fiction Honor Book
Horn Book Fanfare
Coretta Scott King Honor Book
Jane Addams Honor Book
New York Times Best Books for Children and Young Adults
Buxtehude Bulle Award (West Germany)
Best of the Best Books, 1970–1983

Let the Circle Be Unbroken (1981)
ALA Notable Book
ALA Best Books for Young Adults
Coretta Scott King Award
New York Times Outstanding Book
Notable Children's Trade Books in the Field of Social Studies
American Book Award Finalist
Jane Addams Honor Book

The Friendship (1987)
Coretta Scott King Award
Boston Globe/Horn Book Award

The Gold Cadillac (1987)
Christopher Award
New York Times Notable Book

The Road to Memphis (1990)
Coretta Scott King Award
Best Books for Young Adults
ALA Notable Book

Mississippi Bridge (1990)
Christopher Award
Jane Addams Honor Book

The Well (1995)
ALA Notable Book
Parenting Reading Magic Awards Certificate of Excellence for Distinguished Achievement in Children's Literature
ALA Quick Picks for Reluctant YA Readers
Notable Children's Trade Books in the Field of Social Studies
New York Public Library's 100 Titles for Reading and Sharing
New York Public Library's Books for the Teen Age
American Bookseller Pick of the Lists
National Christian Schools Association Lamplighter Award
IRA-CBC Teachers' Choices
Jane Addams Award

Notes and References

1. Mildred D. Taylor: "The Only One"

1.   Mildred D. Taylor, "Mildred D. Taylor," in *Something about the Author: Autobiography Series,* vol. 5, ed. Adele Sarkissian (Detroit: Gale Research, 1988), 268; hereafter cited in text as *SAAS.*

2.   Mildred D. Taylor, "Growing Up with Stories," *Booklist* (1 December 1990): 740; hereafter cited in text as *Booklist.*

3.   Mildred D. Taylor, "Newbery Medal Acceptance," *Horn Book Magazine* 53, no. 4 (August 1977): 403; hereafter cited in text as "Newbery."

4.   Mildred D. Taylor, "Acceptance of the *Boston Globe/Horn Book* Award for *The Friendship,*" *Horn Book Magazine* 65, no. 2 (March/April 1989): 179–80; hereafter cited in text as *Boston Globe.*

5.   Mildred D. Taylor, "Mildred D. Taylor," 11 September 1996 <http://www.penguin.com/usa/childrens/bios/taylor.htm> (11 December 1996); hereafter cited in text as Penguin.

6.   Unless otherwise cited, information and quotations from Mildred D. Taylor come from interviews, telephone conversations, and personal correspondence with the author.

7.   Phyllis J. Fogelman, "Mildred D. Taylor," *Horn Book Magazine* 53, no. 4 (August 1977): 412; hereafter cited in text.

2. Becoming a Writer: A Family's— and Father's—Influence

1.   Sharon L. Dussel, "Profile: Mildred D. Taylor," *Language Arts* 58, no. 5 (May 1981): 604.

2.   Mary Turner Harper, "Merger and Metamorphosis in the Fiction of Mildred D. Taylor," *Children's Literature Association Quarterly* 13, no.1 (1988): 77.

3. Mildred D. Taylor, *Roll of Thunder, Hear My Cry* (New York: Dial Books for Young Readers, 1976), author's note; hereafter cited in text as *Thunder*.

4. Mildred D. Taylor, *Let the Circle Be Unbroken* (New York: Dial Books for Young Readers, 1981), 91; hereafter cited in text as *Circle*.

5. Mildred D. Taylor, *The Road to Memphis* (New York: Dial Books for Young Readers, 1990), 104; hereafter cited in text as *Memphis*.

3. Historical Context: Mississippi and the Civil Rights Movement

1. Mildred D. Taylor, "Acceptance Speech for the 1997 ALAN Award," *ALAN Review* 25 (Spring 1998): 3; hereafter cited in text as *ALAN*.

2. Milton Meltzer, *The Black Americans: A History in Their Own Words* (New York: Harper & Row, 1987), 3; hereafter cited in text.

3. Thomas C. Holt, "Black Americans," in *Collier's Encyclopedia, 1998* (multimedia edition); hereafter cited in text.

4. Carl Sandberg, *Lincoln: The War Years*, vol. 1 (New York: Harcourt Brace and Company, 1939), 574.

5. Sanford Wexler, *The Civil Rights Movement: An Eyewitness History* (New York: Facts on File, 1993), 2; hereafter cited in text.

4. "Will the Circle Be Unbroken?": The Logan Family Saga

1. Ada R. Habershon and Chas. H. Gabriel, "Will the Circle Be Unbroken?" in *Your Gospel Singer,* ed. Edward MacHugh, (1907; reprint, Winona Lake, Ind.: Dallmact Co., 1954), 119.

2. Mildred D. Taylor, *Song of the Trees* (New York: Dial Books for Young Readers, 1975), 49; hereafter cited in text as *Trees*.

3. Anita Silvey, review of *Song of the Trees, Horn Book Magazine* 51, no. 4 (July/August 1977): 384.

4. Review of *Song of the Trees, Booklist* 71, no. 22 (15 July 1975): 1193.

5. Review of *Roll of Thunder, Hear My Cry, Kirkus Reviews* (15 September 1976): 1041.

6. Sally Holmes Holtze, review of *Roll of Thunder, Hear My Cry, Horn Book Magazine* 52, no. 6 (December 1976): 627.

7. Ethel Heins, review of *Let the Circle Be Unbroken, Horn Book Magazine* 58, no. 2 (April 1982): 173–74.

8. June Jordan, "Mississippi in the Thirties," review of *Let the Circle Be Unbroken, New York Times Book Review,* 15 November 1981, 55.

9. Mildred D. Taylor, *The Gold Cadillac* (New York: Dial Books for Young Readers, 1987), 67.

10.   Valerie Wilson Wesley, review of *The Gold Cadillac, New York Times Book Review,* 15 November 1987, 37.

11.   Mildred D. Taylor, *The Friendship* (New York: Dial Books for Young Readers, 1987), 45.

12.   Michael Patrick Hearn, review of *The Friendship, New York Times Book Review,* 21 February 1988, 33.

13.   Anna DeWind, review of *Mississippi Bridge, School Library Journal* 36, no. 11 (November 1990): 120.

14.   Thomas Alpheus Mason and William M. Beaney, "Constitution of the United States: A Commentary; 'Rights of Individuals, Separate But Equal,' " *Collier's Encyclopedia, 1998* (multimedia edition).

15.   Joel D. Chaston, *"The Road to Memphis,"* In *Beacham's Guide to Literature for Young Adults,* vol. 8, ed. Kirk H. Beetz (Washington, D.C.: Beacham Publishers, 1994), 3891.

16.   Mildred D. Taylor, *The Well* (New York: Dial Books for Young Readers, 1995) 9; hereafter cited in text as *Well.*

17.   Marie Orlando, review of *The Well, School Library Journal* 41, no. 2 (February 1995): 100.

18.   Mary B. Burns, review of *The Well: David's Story, Horn Book Magazine* 41, no. 4 (July/August 1995): 461–62.

19.   Deborah Kutenplon and Ellen Olmstead, *Young Adult Fiction by African American Writers, 1968–1993* (New York: Garland Publishing, 1996), xxviii; hereafter cited in text.

20.   Joel Taxel, "The Black Experience in Children's Fiction: Controversies Surrounding Award Winning Books," *Curriculum Inquiry* 16, no. 3 (1986): 273.

5. Taylor's Two Themes: Family and Land

1.   Rosellen Brown, "Starting From Great Faith, Miss.," review of *The Road to Memphis, New York Times Book Review,* 20 May 1990, 48; hereafter cited in text.

2.   *Meet the Newbery Author: Mildred Taylor,* prod. Miller-Brody, American School Publications #004614, 1991, videocassette.

3.   Anita Moss, "Mildred D. Taylor," in *Writers of Multicultural Fiction for Young Adults: A Bio-Critical Sourcebook,* ed. Daphne M. Kutzer (Westport, Conn.: Greenwood Press, 1996), 404.

6. Learning about America:
A Growing Awareness of Racism and Inequality

1.   *Mildred D. Taylor: Roll of Thunder, Hear My Cry,* videocassette. Films for the Humanities and Sciences, #2800. 1988; 1991 release, videocassette; hereafter cited in text as Taylor Video.

2.   Review of *The Friendship, Wilson Library Bulletin* (March 1988): 42.

3.   David Rees, "The Color of Skin: Mildred Taylor," in *The Marble in the Water* (Boston: Horn Book, 1980), 108.

4.   Karen Patricia Smith, "Taylor, Mildred D.," in *Twentieth-Century Young Adult Writers,* ed. Laura Standley Berger (Detroit: St. James Press, 1995), 636.

7. Balancing Reality and Hope

1.   Karen Patricia Smith, "A Chronicle of Family Honor: Balancing Rage and Triumph in the Novels of Mildred D. Taylor," in *African-American Voices in Young Adult Literature: Tradition, Transition, Transformation* (Metuchen, N.J.: Scarecrow, 1994), 248; hereafter cited in text .

Selected Bibliography

Primary Sources

Novels

Roll of Thunder, Hear My Cry. New York: Dial Books for Young Readers, 1976. Paperback.
Let the Circle Be Unbroken. New York: Dial Books for Young Readers, 1981. Paperback.
The Road to Memphis. New York: Dial Books for Young Readers, 1990. Paperback.
The Well. New York: Dial Books for Young Readers, 1995. Hardcover.

Novellas

Song of the Trees. New York: Dial Books for Young Readers, 1975. Paperback.
The Gold Cadillac. New York: Dial Books for Young Readers, 1987. Paperback.
The Friendship. New York: Dial Books for Young Readers, 1987. Paperback.
Mississippi Bridge. New York: Dial Books for Young Readers, 1990. Paperback.

Speeches and Autobiographical Writings

"Newbery Medal Acceptance." *Horn Book Magazine* 53, no. 4 (August 1977): 401–9.
"Mildred D. Taylor." In *Something About the Author Autobiography Series,* vol. 5, edited by Adele Sarkissian, 267–86. Detroit: Gale Research Company, 1988.
"Acceptance of the *Boston Globe/Horn Book* Award for *The Friendship.*" *Horn Book Magazine* 65, no. 2 (March/April 1989): 179–82.
"Growing Up with Stories." *Booklist* (1 December 1990): 740–41.

"Acceptance Speech for the 1997 ALAN Award." *ALAN Review* 25 (Spring 1998): 2–3.

Secondary Sources

Biographical Essays and Literary Criticism

Chaston, Joel D. *"The Road to Memphis."* In *Beacham's Guide to Literature for Young Adults,* vol. 8, edited by Kirk H. Beetz, 3890–97. Washington, D.C.: Beacham Publishers, 1994. Provides a brief overview of Taylor's life and works and a useful critical analysis of *The Road to Memphis.*

Dussel, Sharon L. "Profile: Mildred D. Taylor." *Language Arts* 58, no. 5 (May 1981): 599–604. An early review and biography of Taylor.

Fogelman, Phyllis J. "Mildred D. Taylor." *Horn Book Magazine* 53, no. 4 (August 1977): 410–14. Some personal insight into the life of Taylor written by her longtime editor and friend. Provides some biographical information not found in any other source.

Harper, Mary Turner. "Merger and Metamorphosis in the Fiction of Mildred D. Taylor." *Children's Literature Association Quarterly* 13, no. 1 (1988): 75–80. Another often-cited reference on Taylor. Analysis places Taylor's work in the context of themes and traditions of contemporary African-American literature.

Kirk, Suzanne Porter. "Mildred Delois Taylor." *Writers for Young Adults,* vol. 3, edited by Ted Hipple, 273–82. New York: Scribner's, 1997. A useful survey and analysis of Taylor's novels.

Kutenplon, Deborah, and Ellen Olmstead. *Young Adult Fiction by African American Writers, 1968–1993.* New York: Garland Publishing, 1996. A comprehensive critical annotated bibliography of young adult fiction and nonfiction written by African-American writers, including Mildred D. Taylor. In addition to the annotations, the book has a historical introduction and three helpful appendices that list publication dates and awards.

"Mildred D(elois) Taylor." In *Children's Literature Review,* edited by Gerard J. Senick, 223–29. Detroit: Gale Research Company, 1985. A general overview of Taylor's work followed by excerpts from important reviews of her books from 1975 to 1982.

"Mildred D(elois) Taylor." In *Contemporary Literary Criticism,* edited by Sharon R. Gunton, 418–21. Detroit: Gale Research Company, 1982. A general overview of Taylor's work presented in excerpts from reviews and critical articles published about the author from 1975 to 1978. Includes a long excerpt from Taylor's Newbery Award acceptance speech.

Moss, Anita. "Mildred D. Taylor." In *Writers of Multicultural Fiction for Young Adults: A Bio-Critical Sourcebook,* edited by Daphne M. Kutzer, 401–13. Westport, Conn.: Greenwood Press, 1996. A thorough and perceptive discussion of Taylor's life and works, with a special emphasis on the interconnecting themes of her books. This article covers all of Taylor's books up to *The Road to Memphis.*

Rees, David. "The Color of Skin: Mildred Taylor." In *The Marble in the Water,* 104–13. Boston: Horn Book, 1980. One of the most oft-cited articles about Taylor. It presents a perceptive discussion of why *Roll of Thunder, Hear My Cry* is superior to other novels published about racism.

Smith, Karen Patricia. "A Chronicle of Family Honor: Balancing Rage and Triumph in the Novels of Mildred D. Taylor." In *African-American Voices in Young Adult Literature: Tradition, Transition, Transformation,* 247–76. Metuchen, N.J.: Scarecrow, 1994. A brilliant examination of theme in Taylor's novels, focusing on the importance of the Logan family's values and their vital role in surviving racism.

———. "Taylor, Mildred D." In *Twentieth-Century Young Adult Writers,* edited by Laura Standley Berger, 635–36. Detroit: St. James Press, 1995. A helpful and concise analysis of all of Taylor's books excluding *The Well.*

"Taylor, Mildred D." *Something About the Author,* vol. 70, Edited by Donna Olendorf and Diane Telgen, 222–26. Detroit: Gale Research Company, 1993. An excellent starting point for research on Taylor's life and her writing. Includes statements from the author, summaries of her books, excerpts from selected reviews, and a bibliography.

Taxel, Joel. "The Black Experience in Children's Fiction: Controversies Surrounding Award Winning Books." *Curriculum Inquiry* 16, no. 3 (1986): 245–81. Discusses the issues related to authentic portrayal of black culture and history by comparing the merits of *Words by Heart* and *Slave Dancer* with *Roll of Thunder, Hear My Cry.*

Walker, Robbie Jean. "*Roll of Thunder, Hear My Cry.*" In *Beacham's Guide to Literature for Young Adults,* vol. 3, edited by Kirk H. Beetz, 1135–43. Washington, D.C.: Beacham Publishers, 1990. Provides a brief overview of Taylor's life and works followed by a critical analysis of *Roll of Thunder, Hear My Cry.*

Black History and Other Sources

Habershon, Ada R., and Chas. H. Gabriel. "Will the Circle Be Unbroken?" In *Your Gospel Singer,* edited by Edward MacHugh. 1907. Reprint, Winona Lake, Ind.: Dallmact Co., 1954. The original song lyrics to a hymn referred to in *Let the Circle Be Unbroken.*

Holt, Thomas C. "Black Americans." In *Collier's Encyclopedia, 1998* (multimedia edition). An excellent and very thorough history of blacks in America, including prominent events, individuals, legal rulings, and political trends.

Meltzer, Milton. *The Black Americans: A History in Their Own Words.* New York: Harper & Row, 1987. Excerpts from primary sources. An excellent and interesting "first-person" history of blacks in the United States.

Payne, Charles M. *I've Got the Light of Freedom: The Organizing Tradition and the Mississippi Freedom Struggle.* Berkeley: University of California Press, 1995. Details the development of the civil rights movement in Mississippi, with a special focus on events in the 1950s and 1960s.

Wexler, Sanford. *The Civil Rights Movement: An Eyewitness History.* New York: Facts on File, 1993. A very accessible and chronological overview of the civil rights movement. Each chapter includes direct quotations from a number of relevant primary sources that correspond with key people and events in the movement.

Reviews

SONG OF THE TREES

Martin, Ruby. Review of *Song of the Trees. Journal of Reading* 20, no. 5 (February 1977): 433–35.

Review of *Song of the Trees. Booklist* 71, no. 22 (15 July 1975): 1193.

Silvey, Anita. Review of *Song of the Trees. Horn Book Magazine* 51, no. 4 (July/August 1977): 384.

ROLL OF THUNDER, HEAR MY CRY

Fritz, Jean. Review of *Roll of Thunder, Hear My Cry. New York Times Book Review,* 21 November 1976, 62.

Holtze, Sally Holmes. Review of *Roll of Thunder, Hear My Cry. Horn Book Magazine* 52, no. 6 (December 1976): 627.

Review of *Roll of Thunder, Hear My Cry. Kirkus Reviews,* 15 September 1976, 1040–41.

LET THE CIRCLE BE UNBROKEN

Heins, Ethel. Review of *Let the Circle Be Unbroken. Horn Book Magazine* 58, no. 2 (April 1982): 173–74.

Jordan, June. "Mississippi in the Thirties." Review of *Let the Circle Be Unbroken. New York Times Book Review,* 15 November 1981, 55.

THE FRIENDSHIP

Hearn, Michael Patrick. Review of *The Friendship. New York Times Book Review,* 21 February 1988, 33.

Review of *The Friendship. Wilson Library Bulletin* (March 1988): 42.

THE GOLD CADILLAC
Wesley, Valerie Wilson. Review of *The Gold Cadillac. New York Times Book Review,* 15 November 1987, 37.

THE ROAD TO MEMPHIS
Brown, Rosellen. "Starting From Great Faith, Miss." Review of *The Road to Memphis. New York Times Book Review,* 20 May 1990, 48.

MISSISSIPPI BRIDGE
DeWind, Anna. Review of *Mississippi Bridge. School Library Journal* 36, no. 11 (November 1990): 119–20.

Roback, Diane, and Richard Donahue. Review of *Mississippi Bridge. Publishers Weekly,* 27 July 1990, 234.

THE WELL
Burns, Mary B. Review of *The Well: David's Story. Horn Book Magazine* 41, no. 4 (July/August 1995): 461–62.

Orlando, Marie. Review of *The Well. School Library Journal* 41, no. 2 (February 1995): 100.

Videocassettes

Meet the Newbery Author: Mildred Taylor. Produced by Miller-Brody. American School Publications #004614, 1991. Videocassette. An interview with Taylor at her home. Taylor shares photos and stories of her family and discusses how those stories inspire her writing. This videotape is the most recent of the only two available on Taylor.

Mildred D. Taylor: Roll of Thunder, Hear My Cry. Films for the Humanities and Sciences #2800, 1988; 1991 release. Videocassette.

Web Site

"Mildred D. Taylor." 11 September 1996. <http://www.penguin.com/usa/childrens/bios/taylor.htm> (11 December 1996).

Index

The Author

Chris Crowe is a professor of English at Brigham Young University, where he teaches courses in adolescent literature, English education, and creative writing. Before coming to BYU, he taught for four years at Brigham Young University—Hawaii, three years at Himeji (Japan) Dokkyo University, and ten years at McClintock High School in Tempe, Arizona. He earned a B.A. in English from BYU and a master's and doctorate in English education from Arizona State University. He has served as a member of the Board of Directors of the Assembly on Literature for Adolescents (ALAN) and as president of the Utah Council of Teachers of English and has been an active member in the NCTE and other professional organizations. In addition to a novel and two collections of essays, he has edited a collection of short stories for teenagers and has published articles on various topics in *English Journal,* the *ALAN Review, SIGNAL,* and other professional journals. He lives in Provo, Utah, with his wife, Elizabeth, and their four children: Christy, Jonathan, Carrie, and Joanne.

The Editor

Patricia J. Campbell is an author and critic specializing in books for young adults. She has taught adolescent literature at UCLA and is the former Assistant Coordinator of Young Adult Services for the Los Angeles Public Library. Her literary criticism has been published in the *New York Times Book Review* and many other journals. From 1978 to 1988 her column "The YA Perplex," a monthly review of young adult books, appeared in the *Wilson Library Bulletin*.

She now writes a column on controversial issues in adolescent literature for *Horn Book* magazine, "The Sand in the Oyster." Campbell is the author of five books, among them *Presenting Robert Cormier* (Boston: Twayne, 1989), the first volume in the Twayne Young Adult Authors Series. In 1989 she was the recipient of the American Library Association Grolier Award for distinguished achievement with young people and books.